RAISE YOUR VOICE

"Today's complacency is tomorrow's captivity. There is no such thing as silent Christianity. Accordingly, just like the prophet Elijah and John the Baptist in their respective generations, Myles Rutherford is one of the most anointed and truth-telling voices alive today! Pastor Myles embodies the following: truth must never be sacrificed on the altar of expediency. It's time to go raise our voices! This book is not a must-read, it is a must-do."

—**Samuel Rodriguez,** president, National Hispanic Christian Leadership Conference

"*Raise Your Voice* is a book for our time. Never before have the torrents of Hell been met by so deadly a silence as the time we find ourselves in today.... In the midst of the echoes of people reposting what's popular, Myles has opted to travel the lonely road of truth-telling.... What I love most about the book is his intention to raise other prophetic voices around the world who will stand up for what is right. I highly recommend this book and its author. He is a man who lives what he says and says what he lives."

—**Tomi Arayomi,** founder, RIG Nation

"Some books carry more than a good message—they carry the author's life message. *Raise Your Voice* is one of those books. Myles Rutherford is a modern-day John the Baptist, a remnant voice, a revival maker, a burning and blazing torch who lives to prepare the way for an outpouring of God's Spirit. The words in this book are alive with the Spirit of God to compel every reader and every believer to rise up and speak out. As you devour this book, you will be unable to remain silent, and you, too, will become one of God's remnant voices in a desperate hour on this earth."

—**Brian Bolt,** pastor, CityReach Church, Whittier, California

"*Raise Your Voice* is not a book intended to make us feel cozy. It is the beacon from a lighthouse to warn and help us navigate dangerous waters! Thank you, Pastor Myles Rutherford, for your strength and conviction. You address a people who don't even blush at their sin (Jeremiah 6:15)."

—**Joseph and Yolanda Morgan,** pastors, Celebration of Life Church, Nashville, Tennessee

"This book is about being a voice for God in a society that is moving away from Him. It encourages readers to speak out with truth and love, using their God-given authority and faith to make a difference in the world. It also discusses the challenges and rewards of being a voice for God and the impact that believers can have in bringing about repentance and revival."

—**Vladimir Savchuk,** pastor, HungryGen Church, Pasco, Washington, and author of *Break Free*

"This is a book for everyone who truly wants to fear God more than they fear man. In every generation, God raises prophets who declare the Word of God without fear or compromise. Myles Rutherford is one of these in our day. When I hear this man's voice, I hear God's Word. In the midst of the words in this book, I hear God's voice. I'm praying this book gets into every hand that needs it and stiffens the spine of every person who reads it."

—**Mark Varughese,** senior leader, Kingdomcity

"The greatest danger to our nation is not a loud devil, it's a quiet Church. Pastor Myles Rutherford has issued a clarion call for those within the Body of Christ to find their voice and use it to push back the agenda of Hell and release the power and plan of God in the earth. Read this book and know THE REMNANT IS RISING!"

—**Jim Raley,** founder and senior pastor, Calvary Christian Center, Ormond Beach, Florida

"My friend, Myles Rutherford, teaches us that God reveals Himself and works through determined yet daring people—those not afraid to be loud and heard when most prefer to just be quiet and unseen. RAISE YOUR VOICE!"

—Jamie Tuttle, pastor, Dwelling Place Church, Cleveland, Tennessee

"In the beginning when there was nothing, God spoke, and everything came into existence—thus establishing the power and authority of the spoken word. While on the earth, Jesus told His followers (and us) that anything He did, we could do and 'things greater than this,' solidifying that the same power in the spoken word from Heaven exists in the mouth of every believer who is aligned with God. Pastor Myles is anointed of God to rally the remnant of our generation to walk in the fullness of our apostolic authority. You will be encouraged and empowered through his new book, *Raise Your Voice*."

—Tony Suarez, founder, Revivalmakers Ministries

RAISE YOUR VOICE

RAISE YOUR VOICE

AN URGENT CALL TO SPEAK OUT IN A COLLAPSING CULTURE

MYLES RUTHERFORD

SALEM
BOOKS
an imprint of Regnery Publishing
Washington, D.C.

Salem Books™ is a trademark of Salem Communications Holding Corporation.

Regnery® and its colophon are registered trademarks of Salem Communications Holding Corporation.

Cataloging-in-Publication data on file with the Library of Congress.

ISBN: 978-1-68451-469-4
eISBN: 978-1-68451-472-4

Published in the United States by
Salem Books
An Imprint of Regnery Publishing
A Division of Salem Media Group
Washington, D.C.
www.SalemBooks.com

Manufactured in the United States of America

10 9 8 7 6 5 4 3 2 1

Books are available in quantity for promotional or premium use. For information on discounts and terms, please visit our website: www.SalemBooks.com

DeLana, where do I begin? You are the most prized possession of my life. While I could go on and on about your physical beauty, there is much more than that. Even after twenty-seven years with you, I am still consistently amazed by your inner beauty. Your character, love, and dedication to "stand by your man" through thick and lots of thin has spoken volumes to me. I am better because of you. God sent you to me. I love and appreciate your boldness concerning your faith and God. I admire your won't-take-"no"-for-an-answer mindset that challenges my faith for the impossible. I value the authentic identity that you walk in. The slogan that you have coined, "Be you on purpose," is a strong beacon for me and so many who have been touched by it. It only seems natural to dedicate a book about a "voice" to someone whose voice is my favorite to wake up to, listen to, worship with, and talk with. I love you, honor you, value you, and thank you.

I dedicate *Raise Your Voice* to you.

CONTENTS

Foreword

The prophet Isaiah said more than a millennium ago: "Cry aloud, do not hold back; lift up your voice like a trumpet" (Isaiah 58:1 AMP). I chose to follow that instruction and have been lifting up my voice as a Gospel preacher for a half century. After all, silence, as I have said many times, is the language of defeat.

Today, with the proliferation of social media and more outlets for expression than ever, it seems as though everyone is allowed to have a voice—everyone, that is, except Bible-believing Christians. The world may tolerate you as a follower of Jesus as long as you are content to only go to church occasionally and keep your beliefs to yourself. But if you dare to challenge the agendas and activities of a world system that is careening toward destruction, you will be immediately targeted. Legions of people will raise their voices in unison, attempting to shame you and silence your voice, condemn you and discredit your opinions. However, they cannot prevail when believers speak the truth and refuse to cower in silence.

That is exactly why this message by Pastor Myles Rutherford is so important at this critical hour. He is one of my sons in the faith and a proud graduate of Valor Christian College, where he met his beautiful wife, DeLana, who pastors alongside him. Pastor Myles also serves as an overseer for City Harvest Network. God has anointed him to be a voice of revival crying loud in this generation. He is unafraid and unashamed of the true Gospel of Jesus Christ. He proclaims its truth boldly and with conviction. In this book, he encourages every believer to follow his daring lead.

Our world is filled with voices. Most lead only to confusion and conflict. A generation awaits the sound of a mighty voice declaring peace over strife, joy over sorrow, hope over despair, and the sure foundation of faith in God over the shifting sand of human intellects or personalities.

Pastor Myles is called of God and assigned to carry the fire of revival in this hour of desperation. He is a revolutionary, relevant, remnant revivalist who is empowered and anointed to restore a nation, revitalize a civilization, and rescue a generation!

God has also given you a voice. I challenge you to use it—and you can. *Raise Your Voice* will bring you into maximum effectiveness in these final hours of human history.

—Dr. Rod Parsley
pastor and founder, World Harvest Church
Columbus, Ohio

THE VOICE

My parents traveled extensively while my mother was pregnant with me. In her second trimester, she told my dad, "We should name him Myles," because of all the miles they had traveled over the previous few months.

Soon after that, they stopped at a place in Massachusetts called Plymouth Rock. There stood a statue of a man named Miles Standish. This confirmed to them that my name should be Myles. My father was a trumpet player who had always been moved by the music of Miles Davis, so this also seemed to be confirmation.

However, by the time I was born, they had forgotten what they'd decided to name me! So I spent three days in the hospital without a name.

On the third day, a Baptist preacher walked into my mother's hospital room and said, "What are you going to name that child?"

She answered, "We don't know. Right now, he is Baby Rutherford."

The Baptist preacher said, "I think you should name that boy Myles."

The preacher's name happened to be John—so I was officially named by John the Baptist! And by whatever coincidence, I feel that sometimes I have an anointing on my life like John the Baptist's. I feel a strong burden to call God's people into righteousness to prepare them for a "coming back" Messiah!

We are one generation away from becoming a godless society. We need an intervention, a renewal. We need a voice! I pray that you read this book as an *impartation* and not just a collection of information. I pray that as you read it, the Holy Spirit jumps in your belly as a witness and your boldness increases to say what needs to be said in a culture that is bent on canceling the voice of God. Unless a remnant rises at this moment and speaks out, this world will be turned into the Sodom and Gomorrah mentioned in Isaiah 1:9.

Our thoughts are not a threat to the enemy—our *voice* is! God has given us dominion over the earth, according to Genesis 1:26, and He tells us in Hebrews 11 how to use that power. It will require faith. To turn our society back to God, we *must* raise our voices. I will be sharing in this book why you, personally, and the Church, corporately, *must* do so. We are living in a defining moment.

Warning and Disclosure

This is not a motivational book. It's a bold call to respond to a collapsing culture. It's a book meant not only to wake you up, but stir you up. This is not a book intended to be used for church growth. It is not a book about systems, how to pastor, how to win fair-weather converts, or how to influence people, but it is a book about how to speak for God—not how to speak so that people feel inspired or good about themselves, but how to speak on *behalf* of God. I'll explain more what I mean by this, but let me proclaim: This book is meant for *remnant growth!*

This is a book for people who have the Spirit of God invading their hearts. Being a voice for God is sometimes challenging. It makes one misunderstood, unpopular, and often downright lonely. But in the midst of all of those feelings and emotions, the Voices of God find pure joy in completing His agenda. They have peace when they go to bed at night.

God has always looked for people who are willing to do what He needs done. God takes those imperfect people and baptizes them with the passion to do His will. Once so baptized, they cannot escape the clutches of His will. Many examples abound, from Moses to Noah, Samuel, David, and Elijah, and all the way to Peter, Paul, and John the Revelator. These men and women have an intense determination to do God's will. I am specifically attracted to John the Baptist, who the Bible tells us was

"The voice of one crying in the wilderness:
'Make straight the way of the LORD.'" (John 1:23)

What an incredible calling: to be a voice for God. The One who spoke Heaven and Earth into existence and framed the world by His words (Hebrews 11:3) is looking for a mouthpiece on Earth to blow the trumpet!

If the words of God are bottled up in your belly and you are looking for a way to unlock them forth, you've come to the right place.

God has something He wants to say to you and through you!

To keep going, you cannot be fearful. If you accept that you are chosen by God to speak for Him, come hell or high water, feast or famine, then read on.

Preachers, preach on!

God is going to impregnate you with passion to speak for Him. You will feel an intense desire to live rightly, *not* for your own sake, but for others to hear from God. God is looking for His people's trumpets—our mouths—to make a certain sound. This sound that cries out from the remnant voices are shouts of revival. Revival follows repentance. Repentance comes when people speak up about the heart of God. He has voices on this earth ready to speak, ready to bring revival to all creation.

Are you one of them?

I intend to engulf you in the flames of God to the point that you cannot put this message down. It's going to burn out the unresolved chaff that you may unknowingly be carrying. In the chapters ahead, you will see what it takes to be a voice—the cost, the price, the power, and the passion. Becoming a voice is the most rewarding and humbling experience a person can have. May God richly bless you to be a mouthpiece for Him.

CHAPTER 1

PREACHERS, PREACH ON

Cry Aloud, Spare Not, Lift Up Your Voice as a Trumpet

This chapter should not be read sitting down. If you're in a hurry and cramming this chapter in, put the book down and come back later.

First, let me define what a true preacher is. It's not just the person holding the mic on Sunday. Preaching does not follow ordination, it follows salvation.

Mark 16:15 says, "Go into all the world and preach the gospel to every creature." That's the Great Commission. It's not something you puzzle over, try to figure out, or define—no, you *do* it! This commission goes to every person who receives salvation. If God never calls you to hold a microphone and stand in a pulpit, so be it—and if you need that to call yourself a preacher, then you're not a preacher, you're a performer.

God has chosen you to be a voice, and that means being a preacher! Please get it out of your head right now that a preacher is someone who holds a microphone, has a white collar, or has a certificate hanging on the wall in his office.

Two New Testament words are used to describe preaching: *euaggelizo* and *kerusso*. *Euaggelizo* is where we get the word "evangelize," to proclaim the good news. *Kerusso* means "to herald with gravity and authority, to publish and proclaim openly something which has been done; as a town crier might proclaim critical news with passion and authority, bringing eternal conviction to the listener."

The Apostle Paul said he was a *kerusso* preacher, heralding truth with conviction and persuasion.

> [F]or which I was appointed a preacher and an apostle—I am speaking the truth in Christ and not lying—a teacher of the Gentiles in faith and truth. (1 Timothy 2:7)

Paul tells young Timothy to be ready to preach the Word. (That is, *kerusso*.)

> Preach the Word! Be ready in season and out of season. Convince, rebuke, exhort, with all longsuffering and teaching. (2 Timothy 4:2)

John the Baptist came preaching (*kerusso*) the Word.

> In those days John the Baptist came preaching in the wilderness of Judea. (Matthew 3:1)

Jesus went into the synagogues preaching (*kerusso*) the Word.

And Jesus went about all Galilee, teaching in their synagogues, preaching the gospel of the kingdom, and healing
all kinds of sickness and all kinds of disease among the
people. (Matthew 4:23)

Jesus sent the twelve disciples to preach.

"And as you go, preach, saying, 'The kingdom of heaven
is at hand.'" (Matthew 10:7)

The Gospel will be preached to the whole world with authority.

"And this gospel of the kingdom will be preached [*kerusso*]
in all the world as a witness to all the nations, and then
the end will come." (Matthew 24:14)

Jesus said the "end will come" when you hear preaching that
sounds like this. Most people think it means spreading the Gospel
only, but Jesus also defines the conviction of how it should be
preached: with eternal conviction.

Paul, Timothy, Elijah, John the Baptist, Jesus, the two disciples,
all the major and minor prophets, Stephen the first martyr, and
Peter at Pentecost were all *kerusso* preachers!

Preacher, Refuse to Be Quiet

Preacher, you are God's anointing bottle to the earth. Christ—
the anointing, the hope of glory—is in you. You are covered and
dipped in the anointing of God. When you walk, the anointing

should leave marks on the floor. People should smell the anointing oil on your life before you even get to the room they are occupying. They should hear the sloshing of the saturating oil on your life. Then when you speak, that oil turns to fire!

Will it burn out? Never. God tells us that in the time of trouble, if we open our mouths, He will fill them.

> "I am the LORD your God,
> Who brought you out of the land of Egypt;
> Open your mouth wide, and I will fill it." (Psalm 81:10)

Preachers cannot be quiet. God addresses them first by saying, "I brought you out of that bondage." We tend to keep our mouths shut when we live with a bondage mentality. Satan, our enemy, likes to remind us of our past in order to keep us quiet in the present. Reach to your mouth and unbuckle every spiritual muzzle the enemy has put on you. Don't allow anyone to muzzle the Word of God in your mouth. When you tell a Holy Ghost-filled preacher to stop being bold, it's the same as if you were to:

Tell Noah to stop building a boat and say nothing.
Tell Esther to wait outside the king's door.
Tell Elijah there's no need to call down fire.
Tell Stephen not to testify.
Tell Paul not to write any letters.
Tell Daniel to leave the window shut and not to pray.
Tell Jehu to just ride through the city and leave
Jezebel alone.

Tell David to go back home because the sheep are more important than slinging stones at giants.

Tell Shadrach, Meshach, and Abednego to stoop down just a little.

Tell Moses to stay with Jethro.

Tell Paul and Silas to stop singing.

Tell Jeremiah he should stop weeping because he's being a little dramatic.

Tell Abraham to stay at the foot of the mountain with his son.

Tell Jesus not to flip the tables, not to say things like, "Drink My blood," or not to call people hypocrites, whitewashed tombs, vipers, serpents, and blind guides.

It's saying to the bold preacher, the voice of Heaven itself, "For the love of God, please stop using words like 'woe' and using examples like Sodom and Gomorrah for where the world is headed. Cut our hands off? Pluck our eyes out? Repent? Please don't speak in such ways."

Quiet preachers are often confusing preachers. The world outside is shouting to their god so loudly that sometimes, we can barely hear over the opposing loudness. We are not called to stay quiet. Some people may say we need to be considerate, to just get in a word here and there, and God will take care of the rest. These types of people hide in the safe zones. They have no zeal! The only thing worse than zeal without knowledge is knowledge without zeal.

We know this to be true, but are we zealous and enthusiastic about His commandments that are written on our hearts? The world and some of the Church will call speaking loudly about that "radical preaching," but God calls it "righteous preaching." The disciples remembered what the Old Testament psalmist said about the passion of Jesus: "The zeal of your house has eaten me up." It comes from this scripture in the Old Testament:

> Because zeal for Your house has eaten me up,
> And the reproaches of those who reproach You have fallen
> on me. (Psalm 69:9)

The preacher's passion for God's house and His people must consume him like it consumed Jesus. *We must rip a hole in Hell when we raise our voice in righteousness.* We must get to the place where we are insulted by what insults God. If you say "I wanna be like Jesus," then you have very good examples to follow—the disciples, who were eyewitnesses of Jesus walking this earth. He was a violent voice for change. They knew it and spoke of it.

Preacher, preach on!

Preacher, Preach Right and Preach Righteousness

Matthew 24:37 says, "For the coming of the Son of Man (Messiah) will be just like the days of Noah" (AMP). One of the greatest preachers who ever lived was a boat builder. Society mocked him and laughed at him while he spent 120 years building a boat. The world called him names, but God called him a preacher (*kerusso*) of righteousness!

> [God] did not spare the ancient world, but saved Noah, one of eight people, a *preacher of righteousness, bringing*

in the flood on the world of the ungodly. (2 Peter 2:5;
emphasis added)

It's one thing for others to call you a preacher, but what about
when God calls you a preacher? God called Noah that! A voice of
righteousness! Noah preached for 120 years. You would think that if
somebody preached that long, they should have Bible colleges established, churches planted all over the region, thousands of followers,
stadiums full of people listening to them, and world leaders calling
on them. Not Noah. After preaching for 120 years, only seven people
got in the boat with him. He was so passionate about wanting people
saved that God Himself had to shut the door so the boat would float.
Noah was called a preacher. Was he a failure? Not in God's eyes.

Don't get the psychology-laden, business-and-marketing-
strategy preaching of today twisted with the preaching of the
Bible. God used great and renowned men and women to convince,
rebuke, and exhort others, even when the people would not endure
sound doctrine. Be careful: what you call "radical," God may call
"righteous."

In today's world, we define ministerial success in numeric
terms. We think our church isn't as successful as the church down
the road that has five services on Sunday because we only have
one. But the measure of success in the Kingdom is not majority, but
authority! The measure of success in God's house has always been
about anointing, not attendance.

Some count sheep. God counts soldiers.

God is after a voice that will speak for Him, not a "voice of the
people." If truth and righteousness were about numbers, then why
did God take Gideon down to the creek and thin out his army? Why

did God thin out the crowd on the day of Pentecost? We should be careful how we define "success" in preaching today.

I am not against big crowds. What I am against is defining success by attendance. We stifle great pulpit preachers and make them feel inadequate with the handful that God has assigned to them when we act like this. If we don't stop this "how many" mindset, we will snuff out destinies! Imagine if we judged the impact of Noah's preaching by how many got on the ark?

Genesis 6:5 says every imagination and thought was evil right before the flood—pure sin. The people's hearts meditated on sin, but there was a man named Noah who found grace in the eyes of God. While society was bent on ungodliness, just like today, God raised up a preacher. It will always be this way! God raises up a preacher, a town crier, a herald who doesn't care if he steps on toes. True preachers want God's Word upheld.

What should we be hearing today? *Kerusso* preaching like Noah's. A preacher's responsibility is not *how* the people hear, but *that* the people hear. Our goal is not popularity, it's preparation. In the New Testament, Peter raised his voice and preached on the day of Pentecost, and a little while later, Stephen did the same thing. Three thousand people turned to Jesus with Peter, but the crowds who heard Stephen stoned him to death. Same message, *different* ears. Peter preached to a group of people, and Stephen preached to religious leaders; both are recorded as being "cut to the heart." One group repented, and the other gnashed their teeth—and lashed out at Stephen. People are going to hear truth differently, but we must not allow this to compromise what we tell them.

I believe with all my heart that the fancy, good-for-nothing preaching we hear on a regular basis is done. How much more ear-tickling preaching do we have to hear? I'm so tired of the "I impress myself" preachers of today. They have turned preaching into breadwinning instead of soul-winning! We need preachers with a "Noah anointing" to rise up in this generation.

> How then shall they call on Him in whom they have not believed? And how shall they believe in Him of whom they have not heard? And how shall they hear without a preacher? (Romans 10:14)

The future of America and other nations does not rest on the shoulders of the government, teachers, or activists.

It rests on the shoulders of preachers.

There is an ease in the church of Zion today, and it's going to take preachers to draw a plumb line. Amos 8 tells us there was a famine of the *hearing* of the Word—not a famine of the Word of God itself. Where were the preachers? When Amos preached, a great revival began. The Church today has replaced the good and faithful preachers with the gifted and fancy speakers. We do not have a shortage of speakers; we have a shortage of preachers. Yet the preachers are coming—off the mountain, out of the valley, and out of the caves where they have been spending time with God. Why now? Because a King is coming, and a king does not enter the room until a trumpet blows.

> "Cry aloud, spare not;
> Lift up your voice like a trumpet;
> Tell My people their transgression,
> And the house of Jacob their sins." (Isaiah 58:1)

The voice of a preacher is compared to a trumpet, not a flute. We are not called to charm. We are called to sound an alarm.

The trumpet described in Isaiah 58 is a *shofar*. It doesn't make a sound unless someone shows up and blows into it. The Spirit of the Lord, the *ruach*, the blast of breath, the awakening of God, is inside the preacher who is His trumpet.

Preacher, if you have breath, you have a voice! You are called to be God's trumpet! A trumpet—a shofar—decrees, dedicates, defeats, and delivers. When you raise your voice as a trumpet, it should *decree*.

Preacher, Decree a Thing

Joel 2 says, "Blow the trumpet…and sound an alarm…for the day of the LORD is coming." We find this decree in 1 Thessalonians 4:16, "The Lord Himself will descend…with a shout, with the voice of an archangel, and with the trumpet of God." What is the decree? A king is coming!

The dead rise at this type of preaching—spiritually and even physically. It's this violent blasting of the trumpet of your voice that wakes people! It quickens. It raises the dead. Every time a shofar sounded in the Bible, it announced that something was about to change.

Decree!

We need preachers with trumpets in their mouths. Somebody's coming!

Preacher, Dedicate a Thing

Samuel filled a shofar with oil to anoint David to lead God's people. Also, 2 Chronicles 5:12 tells us about a trumpet being used to dedicate the temple to God, and a thick cloud called the *shekinah* glory filled the house. Preacher, dedicate what you say unto the Lord. Whether people listen or not, they will undoubtedly know that a prophet has been among them.

> "As for them, whether they hear or whether they refuse—
> for they are a rebellious house—yet they will know that
> a prophet has been among them." (Ezekiel 2:5)

Preacher, Defeat a Thing

Judges 7:16 tells about a battle fought by Gideon's army. He put a trumpet and a torch in every man's hand. When they blew the trumpets, they defeated the enemy. My goal with you right now is the same. You are going to do to the enemy's camp what Gideon's army did! Our preaching should make the enemy turn and run. I'm sorely convinced that some of the preaching we hear today actually welcomes the enemy right into the pulpit. A preacher's voice should *annihilate* the enemy, ripping him to shreds. *There should be nothing left of the enemy after you preach.*

Preacher, Deliver a Thing

Joshua 6:20 tells us about how the Israelites took over the walled, pagan city of Jericho at God's command: They marched around it once a day for six days, in silence—but on the seventh day, they blew their trumpets and shouted, and the walls collapsed! The preachers came with a trumpet and shout!

You also can take a city with your shout. You can shift economies with your shout. You can destroy walls with your shout. Your shout is like a trumpet that will shift society. Let God's enemies laugh; the walls will still fall. Raise your voice and shout! Deliverance is in your voice, preacher. Shout with such an understanding.

Psalm 100:1 says, "Make a joyful shout!" David knew what it took to get an audience with God. For a message to register in Heaven, it has to be heard on Earth. Our shout and praise have to go beyond the natural. They must find their way to the spiritual realm. Preacher, I'm telling you, there's an anointing on your shout. We can't be cute in the pulpits or cute in the pews. Joshua shouted before the walls came down. Paul and Silas sang loudly before the prison doors swung open. Jehoshaphat praised loudly before the enemy was destroyed. Why would we stop shouting? Our shout delivers us.

I watch football teams, rugby teams, and other sports teams go out on a field with a shout. We sit in the stands and shout with them, take our shirts off, and paint our faces with symbols and slogans. Then we come to church and sit quietly. How about we praise our God harder and louder than the heathen praises his? Our shout must be turned up a hundred times, even a thousand! Just like in Psalm 100, when we shout, we deliver a thing. *Preachers, preach on!*

We have been entertained and captivated by so-called "relevance." Those days are over! We have become irrelevant because we are more concerned about who we don't offend than the One we represent. If sin doesn't bother you, God is not in you! Preachers are called to represent God, not the people. We should be filled with convictions and courage. There has never been a better time for Holy Ghost preachers in the pews and in the pulpits to raise their voices. We are not just congregants. First, we are soldiers, servants, and preachers. We are not part of a political organization. We are militant, battle-oriented soldiers who endure hardship and are not entangled with the affairs of this life.

The Church should be a dreadful army. The Church should be powerful and unafraid to fight for the standards in which we believe. When preachers rise up, the world will listen. Our voice must be the clarion call that the prophets Joel and Isaiah spoke of. It must be a trumpet.

Prepare the way. The Second Coming of Jesus will be *preceded* by the second coming of preachers! We are not waiting for God. God is waiting for us.

Revival or Resignations

God spoke clearly to me on this point: He is calling for resignations in this season. He's downright firing people who say they represent Him but do not. These playful preachers in pulpits across the nation are being dealt with by a righteous God. If you don't get it right, God will snuff out your voice! If our preaching does not distinguish sin, it certainly won't extinguish it. We cannot afford to embrace sin and opinions when we're called to embrace salvation and holy doctrine.

> Some ungodly people have wormed their way into your churches, saying that God's marvelous grace allows us to live immoral lives. The condemnation of such people was recorded long ago, for they have denied our only Master and Lord, Jesus Christ. (Jude 1:4 NLT)

How many twerking, Hennessy-drinking, vulgar-living, side-bae-having, homosexuality-affirming preachers and so-called worship leaders will we continue to follow? They don't even hide it anymore. I've never seen the Holy Spirit lead a person to drink and party as an expression of grace. I've never seen so many churches open up their services with Drake, Taylor Swift, Beyoncé and other ungodly music to get people to attend. If you have to do this, you're not a pastor, you're a DJ. Stop. We have become a laughingstock to the enemy. The world needs preachers of righteousness!

God has no need for those merely playing the role of preachers and worshipers. For a time, He has given these sorts an opportunity to repent. Many were reluctant to do so because of their pride and position. Therefore, a new wave of God's sovereignty is sweeping over the nation to cleanse His House. He's raising up a new regime of *fire-branded preachers*. They are full of the Word and Spirit. I prophetically forewarn the Church: do not be disillusioned by exposure and driving out of ungodly, selfish, seeker-driven preachers in name only.

Are you one of them? Every preacher who is either living in sin or condoning it—check your integrity. Repent and get back to preaching the powerful Word of God that brings revival to the nation. If you will not or cannot, plan your resignation. I don't care how big your church is, how many followers you have on social media, or how much you jump, shout, and dance. If God's fire has gone out of your preaching because of personal sin, repent or leave—or God Himself will expose you. Preachers have no business cuddling up with sin. Say "no" to compromise! This world needs Jesus, and they can't hear about Him through weak, watered-down preaching. Soft sermons produce soft saints.

A rightly divided Word will never produce a wrongly divided Church. If it smells like compromise, don't go near it. Don't concede the call of God on your life, and don't give the devil one inch.

Why Preach So Hard, Preacher?

In ten to fifteen years, our children will either eat the fruit of our weakness or the fruit of our strength, regardless of whether the fruit is served at church or at home. The morality of any nation rises when preachers preach with conviction and clarity. We must preach sanity, righteousness, repentance, and conversion. Our children need preachers! We are always one generation away from being a godless society. Never before have we so desperately needed preachers to raise a standard. We need preachers who proclaim "hell is hot," "heaven is real," "sin is wrong," and "the Bible is the true Word of God." Our pitiful definition of soft "grace preaching" has led to lawless living, which will in turn set up a lawless society that will lead to a lawless leader called the Antichrist. The only thing that restrains the Antichrist is the Holy Spirit. The only way the Holy Spirit touches our nation is when great preachers, men and women, in the family home and in God's house, stop the deception and start preaching!

Preachers Don't Choose Sides, They Choose God

Preachers are not asking for approval or looking for popularity. True preachers are not a voice for the evangelical right or the liberal left, but a voice for the remnant of God. The world is looking to a political party; God is looking for a people. True preachers are not into white supremacy or black power. We stick to the Word and separate ourselves from the world because we are a voice for God. We are remnant preachers. We preach with conviction and demonstration. We preach grace and truth. We preach that abortion is wrong, and truth and justice is of God. We cannot be bought, and we refuse to be silent.

I'm on the side of righteousness, holiness, and sanctification. This world needs preachers of righteousness. God isn't looking for a church of a certain color. He's not looking for a certain denomination. He's not coming for a political party. He's coming for a delivered church and a chosen people who are called out of darkness. We are in trouble when we think we are called by any name other than God's. "If my people, called by my name" is what He said! The American Church needs a bath of humility. You are a *Christian* first. Not black or white, brown or red.

You are His Church.

We must be politically incorrect right now as preachers!

Preacher, Hold Nothing Back

When the fire of God begins to touch you, you cannot hold back. Jeremiah said it's like "a burning fire shut up in my bones." But he also tells us why it feels like that.

> If I say, "I will not remember Him or speak His name anymore," then my heart becomes a burning fire shut up in my bones. And I am weary of enduring and holding it in; I cannot endure it nor contain it any longer! (Jeremiah 20:9 AMP)

This type of fire changes you. It's birthed out of consecration. It's a fire that doesn't go out very easily. Hell is afraid of these types of voices. These preachers come with a price-paid anointing. The fire of God in them comes from a place of private separation. The fire of God and the voice of the remnant within them started in their personal lives. It is a refiner's fire, not an incinerator. Preachers have to have *that* fire. Once you get touched by fire, everything else is nothing but smoke and lights.

This furnace of affliction mentioned in Isaiah 48:10 and Psalm 12:6 is when God uses a spiritual fire to create emerging voices to boldly confront immorality. Isaiah knew of this all too well. This fire is the glory of God touching your lips, just like the angel who took a tong and placed a coal upon Isaiah's lips. The furnace of affliction lights up ordinary men and women with power produced by personal conviction. It's the same fire you find in Acts 2: It's the fire of the Holy Ghost.

John the Baptist said, "I baptize you in water, but there is One coming who will baptize you with the Holy Spirit and with fire." Something's going to get on you and burn through to the inside of you, preacher! When the Holy Ghost descended, the fire fell. The origination point of the Church of Jesus Christ could very well appear to be drunk, staggering people who would not shut up. The book of Acts does not depict an early church, but the *only* Church. We must stop redefining it and start operating in it!

Suddenly, a fire began that wouldn't go out. It's still not out! People will say it's out. They say a lot of things. But there are preachers on the earth right now—*you*—who keep the fire on the altar! Peter, who denied Christ, began to preach with boldness. Acts 4:31 says *everybody* at Pentecost started preaching with boldness. Stephen, full of faith and power, preached with boldness. Saul, who was a murderer, became Paul and then preached with power and authority, casting out devils, healing the sick, and raising the dead.

It was Paul who told Timothy to stir up the gift of God inside him. The word "stir" in the Greek is *anazopureo*. It means to pour fresh fuel on the dying embers of a fire, to rekindle the flame and fan it! Paul didn't say to wait for Him to stir it up. He told Timothy, "*You* stir up that gift." Don't you dare let that fire go out in your life! A fire cannot sustain itself. You must keep yourself on the altar, a fresh sacrifice for God to use.

Preacher, don't let people say you are too young, too old, or don't fit in. Stop moping and complaining about who does not recognize you, and set yourself on fire! We lose the fire when we fear the enemy and do not fear God. The fear of God is the reverence that drives you to His Word for every answer. Without this healthy reverence, we will look outside the Word for the answers to our questions.

I rebuke the fear that paralyzes and extinguishes the fire of God. It is the fear of people, the fear of rejection, and the fear of failure. Preacher, call down fire from Heaven and burn the gates of Hell.

Preach to yourself first. If the message didn't convict you, it's not going to convict anybody else. We must stop altering the Word of God. We are tellers, not tailors. We are not here to tailor-fit the Word to people's lifestyles. God needs representatives, not law-makers. Preaching the Gospel is meant to help people know how to live godly lives and make godly choices. The lack of biblical preaching that causes people to confront their sin is disturbing. I am burdened that the Church is not burdened. This sin-sick society needs preachers of righteousness. When the Church draws a definitive line, stands up, and becomes what God intended it to be, then the world will sit down and listen.

Preachers, preach on. Don't you dare quit. God is calling you, and the world needs what you have to say. Don't water down what God has called you to speak about. Use clear and concise words. Preach with the sound of a trumpet blowing. When people leave a conversation with you, they are either going to be closer to the cross or driven from it, but your words must not leave them in a neutral position.

God called John the Baptist "a voice in the wilderness," preaching a message that was not popular then and is certainly not popular now. It will never be popular with the majority—but in the ears of God, it is.

That word "cry" means "intense exclamation." John's voice was so powerful that people came out to the wilderness to hear it. His was preaching that caused people to repent from their ways. This preaching never made people feel good about where they were. It led them to prepare for the coming Messiah.

Our pulpits need to be turned into *push*-pits—*pushing* people toward the cross or away from it, but never letting them stay neutral, ever. It's not preaching that tells people to call in the things they want to have in their lives, but rather calls things out. It separates! This type of preaching may get you thrown in jail. Will you still preach anyway?

What if the Gospel we preach becomes so unpopular that you're not just carrying a cross, you're actually put on one? What if the Gospel brings persecution? Will you still serve Him? What if it causes you to share a fate with William Tyndale, who got burned at the stake for translating the Bible into English? Being a preacher of righteousness will bring you sleepless nights and small circles of friends. Will you still preach, preacher? What if your pulpit is not a stage but the very ground your feet hit when you wake up? What if all the world is your stage?

We need preachers! Men and women! Come on, Elijah. Come on, Samuel, David, Moses, John the Baptist, Nehemiah, Jeremiah, and Isaiah! We need you to stop the delusional thinking, keep the light of

God burning, take the heads off giants, and keep moving. We need you! We need you to be like Daniel. Open the window and pray. We need you to refuse to be called the son of Pharaoh, to enjoy the passing pleasures of sin. We need you to eat some locusts and wild honey and preach in the wilderness. Preach repentance.

God is looking for the person who will not compromise or back down. These are the ones who are standing while everyone else is bowing. They represent God to the world. They take no credit and give God all the glory. Second Chronicles 16:9 tells us, "the eyes of the LORD run to and fro throughout the whole earth, to show Himself strong on behalf of those whose heart is loyal to Him." Normalized sin must be countered by those who preach righteousness. It is not for the faint of heart.

We must preach repentance. Acts 3:19 tells us it is the key to every move of God. John the Baptist preached, "Repent, for the Kingdom of heaven is at hand." Jesus preached, "Repent, for the Kingdom of heaven is at hand." On the Day of Pentecost, Peter preached, "Repent, for the Kingdom is at hand." Stephen preached, "Repent, for the Kingdom of Heaven is at hand." Paul preached, "Repent, for the Kingdom of Heaven is at hand." Calvin, Martin Luther, Billy Graham, and so many more preached, "Repent, for the Kingdom of Heaven is at hand."

There is no revival without repentance. The nations will not change unless God sends a preacher!

Prepare the way, preacher. The King is coming!

Preach on!

CHAPTER 2

CRY OUT

How a Voice Is Formed

Andrea Bocelli, the famous Italian tenor, spends hours in a holding room before he takes the stage. He practices runs, inflections, and jumping from high to low notes. He is putting a demand on his voice in a private room. Why all the scales and singing babble before he goes on stage? He is warming up. There is a stage waiting for him, but he understands he will need to check all the fundamentals of his voice and muscles before he steps on it. He makes his private time more powerful than his public time.

In the same way, there are some things you must know in order to prepare your voice. Nothing would be more embarrassing or detrimental than going out on stage to share what God has given you and having it be corrupt or off-key.

When you are a voice for God, you desperately seek time to spend alone with Him. You must refuse to rely on a "gift" only. You must hear from God in your private life. I heard the Lord say, "I've got some people being exposed right now who have been warming up for years. They've been in a cave; locked up, learning how to slay giants."

They are on the backside of the desert, unnoticed by man, but they have been with God. They aren't concerned if you are impressed; they're not moved by popularity. They are only concerned with being empowered by the Holy Ghost to boldly raise their voice for the Truth of God. They only care about one thing: pleasing God!

They have an insatiable desire to spend time with God. They will spend hours practicing and waiting so that when God calls on them, they are ready. Just like fine wine, they have been kept in the cellar for years, getting stronger in the dark, ready to be picked by the owner of the vineyard. The cheap wine doesn't take long to develop, but the expensive, fine wine is saved. The Owner pulls them out when a special guest arrives. That special guest is the Holy Spirit.

You can't find these voices, but God can. Remember David? He wasn't invited to stand in the line with his brothers when God sent Samuel to Jesse's house to look for the next king. Yet God found Him. God doesn't pay attention to what man calls "the perfect voices." He is looking for powerful worshipers. When others overlook you, God sees you. He has need of you!

Strong Warning to Churchgoers

Don't be surprised if the next voice doesn't look the way you thought it would. Saul stood head and shoulders above David and had the look of a leader. David was a young and rowdy teenager, but he was a man after God's own heart, worshiping with the sheep and playing harps, writing songs to God and seeking Him. Even the prophetic voice of Samuel looked at the outward appearance at first to determine God's chosen. It seemed like one of David's brothers was about to be chosen king, but God very clearly said He does not choose people by their outward appearance, but rather what is inside their hearts. Be very careful not to overlook a voice because he or she does not fit a typical religious mold.

A voice for God may be someone who wears different clothes than you expect. It may be a woman when you were expecting a man. The voice may have a checkered past but is now absolutely in love with God. Never judge a book by its cover.

On the TV show *The Voice*, contestants sing for four judges whose backs are turned to the stage, ensuring that they have to make a decision about the contestant based solely on the sound of the voice, not what they see. When that voice is hitting strong with the sound they are looking for, the judges will spin around to connect with that person. Sometimes they are shocked because the person's voice doesn't match their package. "Wow, that's who is singing?!" they say.

This happens to my wife all the time. She has a bold, powerful, boisterous voice of depth and conviction. Her voice is riveting and strong, coupled with a vibrato that fills a room. When she opens her mouth to sing, people are caught off guard. Why? She is only five foot two and a half inches tall but sounds like she is ten feet tall. People will often ask, "How can a voice that big come out of someone so small?" Every time DeLana takes a mic to lead people into the presence of the Lord, the authority and anointing on her shifts the atmosphere.

The world will turn around just like the judges on TV when voices appear. This is what a voice does for God! What about getting God Himself up off His chair? Remember Stephen, the martyr?

But he, being full of the Holy Spirit, gazed into heaven
and saw the glory of God, and Jesus standing on the
right hand of God. (Acts 7:55)

The scripture says that Jesus is seated at the right hand of God,
but here, He is standing. *Not only did Jesus turn His chair around,*
He stood up. I am writing this book with the goal of putting such a
voice in you that the heavens open up and back your actions with the
Glory of God! Let God fill your voice with such power and authority
that when you enter a room, He enters with you.

What is the first step to being a voice for God?

There will be a time in your life that you will have something
to say but cannot say it. God will stir you, but you're not permitted
to be on fire yet. You will have vocal cords but not be able to use
them. This is a hard place to be—a place where you have something
to say but God has not authorized people to hear it yet. I live by a
statement God gave me years ago: "Obedience is in our hands, and
timing is in God's." Even Jesus had something to say but didn't say
it to the masses until He came out of the wilderness. When you
become a voice for God, you will have to understand the season
you are in at all times.

No Words in a Womb

Now Mary arose in those days and went into the hill
country with haste, to a city of Judah, and entered the
house of Zacharias and greeted Elizabeth. And it happened, when Elizabeth heard the greeting of Mary,

that the babe leaped in her womb; and Elizabeth was filled with the Holy Spirit. Then she spoke out with a loud voice and said, "Blessed are you among women, and blessed is the fruit of your womb! But why is this granted to me, that the mother of my Lord should come to me? For indeed, as soon as the voice of your greeting sounded in my ears, the babe leaped in my womb for joy." (Luke 1:39–44)

A baby in the womb cannot vocalize! A baby can leap, have hiccups, suck a thumb, hear, sense touch, and do many other things, but it cannot speak. A baby's vocal cords are formed nine to ten weeks into gestation—and so are the fingerprints. Think about how that coincides. *None of us have the same fingerprints, and none of us have the same voice.* I believe our Master Designer and Creator purposely did this. *Your voice must form its identity before you can be trusted to speak on His behalf.*

Your Voice Is Your Fingerprint

Your voice shows your identity. Your voice defines who you are. No one has your voice. Even technology has been designed around this fact. No one can talk to Siri on your phone like you can. It has learned your identity by simply hearing your voice inflection. The program recognizes you. Many children can call out "Dad!" in a room and it will not move me to instant action. But if one of my children calls out "Dad!" I will immediately recognize that child's voice and turn my head. I know the voices of my children.

It is also the same with a parent's voice to a child. When my wife and I call our children's names, they know who is calling and will pay greater attention. My voice carries weight and authority for them.

Hearing and speech impairments typically go together. A baby in the womb is surrounded by amniotic fluid, which impacts the baby's ability to hear clearly. So the strongest voice for a baby in the womb is the mother's, because it resonates deep inside her chest cavity and it is closest to the baby. Many times, when the baby comes out of the womb, begins to cry, and hears the mother's familiar voice, it will soothe the child instantly.

Spiritually, this means the voice of the next generation is deeply impacted by the mothers and fathers of the current generation.

Think about this. What are we saying to the next generation of voices? If our generation does not speak clearly to the next generation on matters concerning righteousness, godliness, and holiness, those children will grow up with a speech impediment. If you cannot hear clearly, you will not speak clearly. What people say is directly impacted by what they hear.

The Bible asks how people can hear without a preacher. I'm asking, how can they hear without a mother? A father? Whoever has your ear shapes your voice.

Concerning Abortion

What psychological damage have we done to the next generation concerning life in the womb—and then outside of it? Preborn children have thoughts and actions. They can even experience the Holy Spirit in the womb. The Bible and science show us clearly that a baby can hear and react to what is being said outside the womb. John the Baptist leaped inside Elizabeth's womb when Mary greeted her. He was filled with the Holy Spirit. John the Baptist was nicknamed "a voice crying out in the wilderness." John was a crier! That's what you do the first time you come out of a womb: You cry! It's the first step in being a voice. Learn how to cry for a generation.

What's really going on spiritually concerning abortion?

How many voices have been snuffed out of this world before they ever had the opportunity to speak? Abortion is one of the most detestable blights upon the nations of this world. It not only wipes out a baby, it wipes out a voice. We as the people of God must wake up and see that the enemy is working very hard to take away the voices of God in the next generation. But God will *always* have a remnant that will speak!

Go Ahead and Cry

Babies don't speak at first. They cry. Did you hear that?!

Doctors expect babies to cry within thirty seconds to one minute after birth; this is necessary for the baby to begin to use his or her lungs to breathe. Before birth, the lungs were dormant because the umbilical cord provided him with fresh oxygen and took carbon dioxide away from his bloodstream.

Once outside the mother's womb, babies' noses and lungs are suctioned to clear them of amniotic fluid and all other secretions, but they also try to clear the clutter from their lungs and noses by crying. Until very recently, babies who did not cry on their own were made to cry by stimulation. For this, the doctors would hold the baby upside down from the feet and spank them on their buttocks.

I believe this is prophetic. God spanks us when we won't cry! He chastises those whom He loves. When a church stops crying, God steps in with correction. That correction typically is a voice that speaks harshly to the Church in order to bring it back to discerning its ways. We need the Church to breathe—so whatever it takes, *breathe!*

In the first stage of your life, you will cry because of the need *to breathe.* Crying is how we first communicate to the world. We always do this when we leave a comfortable position and go to a new place. It's how we transition. My father-in-law always says, "Frustration is a sign that something needs to change." In order to speak in a new setting, the Holy Spirit will awaken you. It may seem frustrating at first because all you will be able to do is cry. You will feel a need to say something, or at least announce that you are ready to leave the comforts of the last season to communicate to the world in this new season. The *baby* is responsible to leave the comforts of the womb, not the mother.

Just as the baby decides the timing of the birth, we decide when we are ready to go to the next level. Just know that the longer you stay in the womb, the more uncomfortable you are making everyone else.

Our first child, Brooklyn, was born two weeks late. The doctor said, "She just does not want to come out of the womb." His next words were powerfully prophetic about where we are as a Church that remains silent: He said if Brooklyn did not come out of the womb, she would die from exposure to her own feces. She had to come out!

The Church today has lost touch with the Great Commission to reach the world by staying inside the womb of the sanctuary! We are too comfortable in our ways. We are so comfortable with our safe zones of "churching it" that we are no longer salt and light.

Our second child, Lyncoln, was born eight weeks early. The doctor said, "We've got to get him out of there, he's squeezing the umbilical cord, then passing out." There's danger in coming out too early as well; Lyncoln's lungs weren't fully developed, so he had to be incubated for weeks in the neonatal intensive care unit.

Today, both our children are extremely healthy and working in full-time ministry. But the first moments of their lives bear a testimony.

The first thing that comes out of the womb is the baby's head. When you come out into a new season, the first thing you have to do is stick your head into that next place. Don't go in backward; that will be painful for you and everybody else involved in the birthing process. The same happens when God is calling you to leave a place of comfort and become a voice for Him. You have to get your head and your thoughts into the new season. It will require a season of crying, of gasping to breathe in a new atmosphere. This crying can only be consoled by somebody whose voice is familiar to you.

If you're going to be a voice for God, you will cry first—period. A burden will fall on you that you don't know what to do with. I remember being in my closet in 2019, bent over with weeping. My wife came in and said, "What's going on?" I said, "I don't know. I've never felt this before."

I wept. I knew God was calling me to become a voice for repentance and clarity, but how? It was different, and I knew that if I did not accept the burden, God would pass me over and put it onto the next person He was seeking for. I told the Lord, "I want it, keep it on me!"

You also will feel a burden for humanity, and you also will feel the heart of God—but at the same time, the only thing you'll be able to do is cry until you figure out how to properly respond to and share that burden. You may respond incorrectly for a while, but say what you are feeling anyway. This struggle helps you develop your voice. That burden is a touch from God. Don't dismiss it. Being burdened has rewards for those who will humble themselves under the mighty hand of God and follow His voice.

Nehemiah had a burden. He wept, he prayed, and he fasted. That's all he knew to do because the burden was so strong. He could not hide it from the king he was serving, and that was not good. He was a cupbearer; his job was to taste the wine to make sure no poison was in it before he gave it to the king. No one who attended the king so personally was allowed to have a sad countenance in his presence, but Nehemiah's was so dramatically different that the king said, "What is wrong with you?"

At that moment, Nehemiah went to the next stage: crying to communicate. This is when we cry to direct attention to a problem. When babies want food, they cry. When they want to be held or pampered, they cry. Before they've learned one word, they just cry.

This period is not supposed to be a long season. If it is, something is not developing correctly. Sometimes a parent will pacify children too long because they are irritated by the crying, but if they reward the crying too long, they will cripple the child's development. The *now* generation must help form the *next* generation's vocabulary and voice. How many adult Christians do you know like this? They will never become a voice in any capacity because all they do is cry. They don't say "Daddy," "Mama," or even "Abba." They only cry when things don't go their way.

I wish I had paid attention in my high school Spanish class. I would be able to speak the language of so many around me! What am I missing out on simply because I didn't allow my teacher to help me develop? I am severely limited in what I can say or do. How many piano lessons did I show up for unprepared because I didn't think it was important to practice? While I can play a few chords now, what would I be able to do now if I had completely given myself over to the teacher?

This is how I feel about the current generation. While we were trying to communicate, many parents stuck us in a room at the church and told us to play videogames while they lifted their hands in faith, believing for miracles but not securing them for us. Then, when we grew into our teenage years, they offered us social hangouts, light shows, entertaining music, and fun activities. They thought that as long as they kept us in the house of God, something was going to change. The Bible is very clear that we are to train up a child in the ways of the Lord, not simply bring them up and drop them off. As we exited our teenage years, the church offered us coffee, one-hour services, a little social group, and an inspirational word saying that God wants the best for us.

The church in general had little to no impact on the other 165 hours of the week. As long as we stay stuck with a pacifier in our mouths, we will never be a voice for God. No, we will be a voice for ourselves. And the same will be true for our children if we don't change things now.

Salvation Army Founder William Booth once said, "If I had my choice, I wouldn't send you to school, I'd send you to Hell for five minutes, and you'd come back real soul winners."[1]

This season of developing the voice to communicate is crucial. Comfort is not good when teaching a child to use his voice to communicate. The two ways to help a child develop his communication skills are to deprive him of what he wants until he starts asking for it properly and modeling speech for him yourself. You tell him, "You don't get what you want by crying, but by speaking. And this is what you say."

In the third stage of life, crying is emotional. Crying is good, don't get me wrong; it's sometimes necessary. It is an emotion of your heart that comes out with hurt or disappointment. You cry because of a death or frustrations. You cry because you are ruled by emotions. We cry at this stage to help cope with all life throws at us. We cry out of a spontaneous reaction to an experience or person that moves us. This is natural.

All of these stages are necessary to develop a *voice!* We cry in desperation to see something that is beyond our ability to make happen, to fix a thing we are incapable of fixing by ourselves. We cry out of conviction to speak on God's behalf to a confused humanity and a compromised Church.

In the fourth stage, you cry spiritually because the need is so great. *This is the weeping stage.* This is the place where a burden becomes so strong that it bucks the religious system of the day. It's a *crier* anointing.

John was a voice crying in the wilderness, and Jesus wept over Jerusalem. Jeremiah was called the weeping prophet. He wrote the Book of Lamentations, which means "weeping."

He also was called to prophesy to Jerusalem about a coming destruction. Why? Because the people had forsaken God. They were killing their children and offering them to Baal. Aborting children. Because of this, God said Judah would suffer famine, plunder, and captivity. Something spiritual became physical and created a need for a prophet to *cry out*. Interestingly, the book of Jeremiah is where we get the scripture that says, "Before I formed you in the womb, I knew you...I ordained you as a prophet to the nations" (Jeremiah 1:5). That scripture alone is foundational for the believer to turn from any support for abortion.

Kill the Babies

When Moses was born, Pharaoh sent out a decree: kill the babies. When Jesus was born, Herod sent out a decree: kill the babies. In Jeremiah's day, God's chosen people were willfully sacrificing babies. Whenever you see a generation supporting babies being killed, you will see deliverers being born! That means the enemy is doing everything he can right now to silence the voices of deliverance for our generation. It also means there are deliverers on the earth right now who walk in the spirit of Moses, Jesus, Jeremiah, and John the Baptist—voices that cry aloud and spare not. Maybe that is why you are reading this book. You were formed in the womb for a reason. You made it through birth, like Moses in the Nile. Isn't it ironic that it was his cry in the Nile that saved his life?

We must see Satan's hand in this. The satanic church is the leading advocate for abortion. That should tell you something. Abortion is Satan's way of snuffing out the next voices of deliverance in that generation. He first steals the voice, then kills the voice, and then destroys the nation that needs to hear the voice.

A voice for God will weep because of a burden for the people. Jesus wept over Jerusalem, "God give them shepherds." Moses interceded many times, "God, spare your people!" A crier anointing is also what we find on Nehemiah, who wrote, "And it came to pass, when I heard these words, that I sat down and wept, and mourned certain days, and fasted, and prayed before the God of heaven" (Nehemiah 1:4 KJV).

Weeping over the issues of the day is certainly a prerequisite for becoming a voice for God. David Wilkerson called it the "Baptism of Anguish." The crier anointing is intercession mixed with a righteous indignation. Righteous indignation is when you are mad about the things that are displeasing to God yet being angry without sinning yourself. To prove this, Jesus wept over the city and then flipped tables the same day. Jesus drove the money changers out with this crier anointing. It's not popular. Just like Jesus, when you become a voice, first you weep, then you whip.

Jesus is love, but to the religious manipulators in His temple, He was a whip-bearing, table-flipping radical and religion-defying madman. Needless to say, He didn't get many invitations to preach in the Temple. The religious leaders wanted His voice quieted. It interfered with the system that brought the money in. The Bible says in Luke 19:48 that they were unable to do anything because all the people were very attentive to hear Jesus's words. What was He going to say next?

Cry! Cry aloud, spare not, and lift up your voice like a trumpet. This generation needs the crying voice of preachers in the wilderness. You're not in the wilderness wandering, you're in the wilderness waiting. God is sending your voice to cry out to a generation and to a nation—but you're going to have to participate. Your voice is the only password that will open up the hearts of people around you. Observation is not an action in the Kingdom; participation is! "The violent take it by force" (Matthew 11:12).

When the disciples asked Jesus when the Kingdom would come, He said that the Kingdom is not observed (Luke 17:20). The Kingdom of God does not work through observation, it works through participation. That means God is looking for people who will raise their voices and partner with His Word for it to move forward. God is raising up your voice like John the Baptist, Jesus, Jeremiah, Nehemiah, and others.

Cry out! Cry out!

CHAPTER 3

THE CHURCH IS IN TROUBLE

*If There Is a Mist from the Pulpit,
There Will Be Fog in the Pews!*

The climate of today's church culture is increasingly tolerant and accepting of sin and redefining the Word of God. We are in trouble! The voices of great men and women who have already gone on to Heaven echo loudly in my ears, and they are more resoundingly present than many of our current preachers concerning the ancient, nearly forgotten boundary stones of our faith: righteousness, godliness, and holiness. Please hear me. I believe that all of us as ministers of the Gospel have different assignments, but I do not believe that means throwing away the standards that hold us accountable to God's Word. I want to address the preachers in the pulpit and then the Church at large. We are one generation away from having our voice completely silenced.

We are in trouble, and we need an immediate intervention.

To the Preachers in the Pulpit

I am aware that this chapter may not sit well with some pastors and "five-fold preachers," but we are in trouble. I am grieved because God grieves! How did we get here? Why are nations living so lawlessly and calling good evil and evil good? What is going to happen if we don't speak up? Are we willing to face persecution for righteousness, or will we continue to preach motivational sermons and keep people numb to the heart of God? We are definitely in a prophetic season right now, and if we don't make some changes concerning what we call "ministry," there may not be anything left for our children's children. Dark ages are ahead if we don't change our perspective on the Church, ministry, and what we call the preaching of the Gospel!

The moral decay in the world didn't start on the streets, but under the steeple! Our pulpit preaching for the last twenty-plus years has been riddled with feel-good motivation, poor copies of TED talks, and story times. Our gatherings have centered around people more than around God—and the people are pampered, political, polished, and possess no moral values.

Recently, I was backstage at a conference where I had been invited to preach and fell into conversation with one of the main speakers. He was astounded that mine is one of those churches that uses words like "conviction" and "repentance." In a similar setting at a different conference where I was preaching, the first thing one preacher talked about wasn't how many people are getting saved in his church's city, but how much money they had. I was floored.

We can wildly miss the mark concerning the true reason we are in the ministry. It has gotten so bad that entire nations are faced with the atrocious sins of abortion, injustice, confusion over sexual orientation, gender identity and transitioning, pedophilia, and other social issues, and very few preachers will whisper a comment about those things for fear of losing members. Shame on us! What are we doing? *Why* are we doing what we are doing? What is the motive behind it, and is it moving anybody toward God? It's hard to preach with a pacifier in your mouth. We need bullhorns in our hands.

Preacher, what is God is going to ask us when we stand in front of Him? "How many members were in your church?" "How much money did you raise?" "How big of a building did you build?" He's not going to say, "Well done. You got those people hyped!" He's not going to say, "Thank you for lowering the standard to make sure many could continue to sin." He's not going to say, "You focused on the length of people's hair and how cleanly shaved they were, long dresses and no jewelry, and called it righteousness. Good job." He's not going to say, "Hey, I'm so grateful that your standard of holiness was that you would not allow people to raise their hands in church." He's not going to say, "Thank you for making sure the people in your pews voted Republican/Democrat." He's not going to say, "Wow, you had over a hundred thousand followers on your social media platforms." And He's not going to say, "Well done, you really entertained those people" or "Great number one hit song!"

No, no, no!

He's going to ask if you were faithful to His Word. He's going to judge your work by that measure.

True ministry is not driven by greed; it's driven by God. If our decisions, preachers, are driven by financial gain, we're not pastors, we are businessmen. I am sorely convinced that what some people call Kingdom Business is really nothing more than hidden entrepreneurship.

We need the Holy Spirit to advance us for God's glory, not ours. One reason the baptism of the Holy Spirit is not preached today is because it's the natural enemy of church marketing. Many sermon series over the last few years have focused more on sex and how to be successful in relationships than on the Spirit of God. If we instead teach conviction, repentance, and the fear of the Lord—if we train our children to take their cues from the Word and not from the world—we will have no reason to preach a sermon series on bedroom antics. We need a fresh fire-and-wind baptism of the Holy Spirit to hit the preachers of America and the nations. Many preachers of today need to go back down in the water and repent for being so passive toward sin.

God wants us to build disciples, not just church memberships. I don't think that is what Jesus had in mind when He said, "I will build My church." His Church isn't the building. If we think of it that way, it proves why there is no power—just a form of godliness—when it comes to demonstrating the Gospel.

With a fresh baptism from the Holy Spirit, we will stop being user-friendly to the people and become more trusted by God. The early Church in the book of Acts had no building, no money, and no political influence, yet the services were producing three thousand to five thousand converts every day! That's exciting to me! I believe we're in a season when things like that are going to happen again—but we're going to have to separate ourselves from everything else and allow God to sift out whatever is mixed in us that is not of Him. Don't call separation "division," and don't call the preaching of righteousness "legalism."

> "Come out from among them And be separate," says the Lord. "Do not touch what is unclean, and I will receive you. I will be a Father to you, and you shall be My sons and daughters," says the LORD Almighty. (2 Corinthians 6:17–18)

We need a complete separation from the world—a scalding bath from it. This theme should be present in our sermons, our worship, our desires, our motives, and our need to be praised by men. We need a blood washing. The decline of morality in the Church, the downward spiral of faithfully gathering with one another, a waning desire to live godly lives and strive for holiness, is the product of the last twenty years of weak preaching! The altars have been taken out, ministers have learned to speak on behalf of the people rather than on behalf of God, and we have downgraded the powerful and penetrating Gospel of Jesus Christ to psychology, sociology, and accepting anything that goes.

No wonder we have rainbow flags flying over church doors! We have made it all about getting a crowd to show up. I am so done with the preaching of today. It's mostly powerless and changes nothing. We are in trouble when the prayer meeting is practically nonexistent and Sunday morning is produced and performed, centered around the people rather than God.

Lights, camera, action? How about prayer, power, and conviction!

When we see the prayer meeting get as big as the Sunday meeting, we will see God move and the revival we say we want actually happen.

Do we want it? Are we willing to shift gears for it? If not, we will remain in trouble.

Weak Preachers Produce Weak Saints

Where are the voices of our generation? Where are the preachers? The John the Baptists, Elijahs, Noahs, Pauls, and Timothys? Where are they? I don't mean motivational speakers, puppeteers, church businessmen, church-growth strategists, or self-help gurus sharing another series on success. Where are the preachers of conviction, repentance, Hell, true salvation with conversion, the Second Coming, and second death, preaching about getting right with God and holding onto the altar until true change happens—preaching with demonstration?

Where are the preachers who hold the sword of the Lord against blatant wickedness that turns the hearts of an entire generation toward lawlessness?

That kind of preaching is unfamiliar to many. I believe there are a handful of people who do it—and thank God for them—but we need more men and women who will not compromise. We must turn away from any mixed messages right now for the sake of preserving the Gospel of Jesus Christ for the next generation.

If you look at the seven churches of Asia Minor that Jesus Himself mentioned in the Book of Revelation, you will see that He is writing to the "angel" of those churches. That means He was dealing with the leadership of every church. The loveless church, the lukewarm church, the church that tolerates Jezebel and sexual immorality—these messages were written not to the whole body of the church, but to their generals! When God wants to deal with the nation, He will deal with the leaders of the Church first. Judgment always begins in the House of the Lord. I truly believe that if we're going to see change in our nation, preachers must return to preaching the unadulterated Word of the Lord. We must abort our silly sermon series, laden with popcorn and snacks, and make our desire relevant to God. We must stop telling ourselves that in order to reach people with the Gospel of Jesus Christ, we have to mix the secular with the sacred. I cannot imagine Jesus headlining a show with Nicki Minaj, Lil Nas X, Drake, Beyoncé, Taylor Swift, Harry Styles, or anyone else in order to draw a crowd. I believe Jesus would have reached out to them to share the Gospel, but I do not believe He ever would have mixed His agenda with theirs. God gave this saying to me many years ago: *Jesus sat with sinners, but He didn't sin with them!* There is no way you can deliver people from something that you're delivering *to* them.

Yes, secular music will probably fill the house with sinners, but they're going to leave the same way they came in. Many preachers and pastors are doing things for the sake of reaching sinners that create a church environment and members who are consumer-minded, not conviction-driven. There is a consequence to that. It's called confusion, false comfort, and lack of conviction. We need preachers to get the fire of God back into the pulpits. That fire comes from the Word of God and nowhere else. I firmly believe we have too many businessmen doing church business rather than preachers preaching God's business.

Preacher, you are the change the world needs to see! God wants us to be so in tune with Him that when we are done preaching, we shut the Bible and carry it with us as we walk off the stage without looking back. If it's the last time those people hear the message, that should be fine. Every time we preach, we must prick their hearts with such conviction that they can't shake off Hell's flames unless they go to the altar and repent. At no time should we make people feel comfortable in their sin.

I am grieved. The Gospel is not the Gospel if it is a gospel of indifference. We have made God familiar. He's our buddy down the street. He's a long-lost friend we can talk to every once in a while. We have preached for too long that God sits up on the throne giving out hall passes for every person who sins.

Don't give an inch! You are watchmen on the wall; you are shepherds caring for the most powerful force on the face of this earth: the people of God. We cannot give up any more ground for the sake of what some will call "church growth."

During the 1980s when I was growing up, we would have church on Sunday morning and then come back on Sunday night. Then we would have a midweek meeting. In addition, we would be involved in service groups on another night. My family and I loved this schedule. We didn't care how long church lasted. We were excited to come back Sunday night and see the Holy Spirit move. On Wednesday night we were excited to hear the teaching of the Word of God. We also showed up on Sunday mornings prior to the service for Sunday school.

Then eventually, many church leaders gave up holding Sunday night services. We just didn't need it because it interrupted family time. We forgot that being in the House of God *was* family time.

Then we gave up the midweek service because people were just too busy to come. They had jobs, and their kids had football and soccer practices.

Slowly we dumbed down the gathering of God's people to an average of one hour and fifteen minutes per week.[1] I thought God said He wanted at least one day set aside to rest from our labor and spend time with Him—but we have found that all *we* desire is one hour! Look at the decline of society because we, the Church, have given up so much ourselves. That one hour and fifteen minutes of preprogrammed songs and sermons most of us are familiar with do very little except drive the members in and out, like cattle getting flea dipped. We are in trouble.

What if God moved at one hour and *sixteen* minutes into the service? Would we wait on the Holy Spirit or dismiss Him?

When someone begins to speak in their heavenly language, will we escort him out to keep from offending people? Will we wait for the Holy Spirit to move, or will we keep our polished performance on schedule?

"Cry aloud, spare not, lift up your voice like a trumpet" (Isaiah 58:1). God calls our voice a *trumpet!* Not a bell to jingle, but a trumpet. A resolute sound that should cause a generation to not only wake up but to *get up.*

If you've read this far, let me encourage you. Preacher, the fire is in you. Victory is in your mouth. You are the mouthpiece of God sent to sound the alarm and declare what true victory looks like. You hear me? It's your time. An alarm is going off in preachers everywhere. Listen to it. It's from God. The preacher's anointing is what will set people free. It's a message for the sinner to *repent* and a call to the Church to *make the crooked places straight.* Jesus is coming back, and He is always going to send voices on the earth that will prepare the way. Preachers, *preach on!*

If Mr. Money comes or goes, preach on.

If Mr. or Mrs. Network comes or goes, preach on.

If Mr. Guru comes or goes, preach on.

If the crowds come or go, preach on.

Whether the building is ever built or not, preach on.

Set yourself on fire and burn! Noah saved seven people plus himself. Philip was sent to just one person. Peter preached under the power of the Holy Spirit, and three thousand people came to know Christ.

Whether you are sent to one or ten thousand, you are sent! You are sent to preach the Gospel. This is your season. This is your time. Paint the canvas right now with your voice—with vivid colors, not fifty shades of gray! Throw back the curtains, put your shoes on, do a Haka war declaration, walk out there, and preach like a wild man set on fire.

I'm speaking to you prophetically. *Don't waste time, don't question God's Word that He's given you, don't second-guess it.*

As for them, whether they hear or whether they refuse—
for they are a rebellious house—yet they will know that
a prophet has been among them. (Ezekiel 2:5)

Miracles and moments of glory wait for you after you preach the Gospel of Jesus Christ. You are different, and you are never going to fit in. You were never designed to fit in. Jesus was "a root out of dry ground" (Isaiah 53:2); this means He didn't take anything from this world in order to do the work of God.

Preach! Don't preach passively, don't preach your political persuasions, but *preach* liberation from sin. Preach liberation that opens prison doors, sets the captives free, and fills them with the Holy Ghost!

To the Church

When you read what Jesus said about you, it should change your life. Jesus said in the red words of Matthew 16:18, "Upon this rock I will build my church, and all the powers of hell will not conquer it" (NLT). Jesus takes complete ownership of the Church. We are a people who belong to the Lord, which means He takes ownership of *us*. We are owned. That is what redemption means: bought back.

As such, you are the most powerful force on this earth. While Satan wants you to think he has power, the Bible specifically says he does not have an ounce! He has been completely disarmed by Jesus's crucifixion and resurrection. He has absolutely no power except influence. That means the only way he can change anybody is through the power of temptation.

Let's define what the word "church" means before we move any further. The word in the Greek is *ekklesia*, which simply means to be called out.

EK – out from the world

KALEO – called

If we are "called out," then from what are we called out? In Matthew 13, Jesus tells the parables about salt, light, seed, and hidden gold. He's talking about things that are in the world but somehow different. We should be seed in Hollywood, seed in politics, seed in the entertainment industry. We are called to be salt.

When people taste us, they should taste something different. When we walk in a room, the atmosphere should change, and the people should feel the presence of God. We have lost that because we want to be popular, not peculiar. The one thing we're not called to do is conform to any worldly environment in which we find ourselves.

First Peter 2:9 says "But you are a chosen generation, a royal priesthood, a holy nation." We are a peculiar people that God has called out of darkness and into His marvelous light. We were once aliens, but now we're the people of God, full of mercy and proclaiming grace and truth.

To live only with the grace of God and not the truth is to receive a failing grade. Living at 50 percent is like only taking half of a test, then handing it to the teacher while hoping you pass. The teacher is going to say, "What about the other half? Are you going to finish that part of the test as well?"

The Church is a group of people who are called out of a worldly system to completely function with a Kingdom mindset.

You cannot be a defining voice in the culture if you sound like and participate in the same foolishness as citizens of the kingdom of darkness. You must be separate!

I like what Myles Munroe used to say: There are two worlds on this one earth. There is a Kingdom of Darkness and a Kingdom of Light. Darkness means ignorance, and light means knowledge.[2]

Darkness denotes ignorance, yes, but the continuing undercurrent of immorality in our churches stems not from the fact that we are ignorant, but that we *willfully* ignore knowledge. You can profess to be in the Kingdom of Light and choose to willfully ignore the source of Light itself. The Bible says that to know something is wrong but to still do it is sin. Sin is a *willful* separation from God. As a disciple of Jesus Christ, we need to reevaluate our choices.

One of my favorite preachers is B. H. Clendennen. He says in a message called "Soldiers": "We're going to have to stop lying to ourselves that we can't stop sinning; that cigarette doesn't jump out of your pocket and light itself."[3] He means that we willfully do things we know are wrong, but we absolve ourselves from responsibility. Those things "just happen."

What has gone wrong with the Church? It has lost much of its power because we got so busy calling things in that we forgot to call things out. "God give *me*…bless *me*…open up the windows of Heaven…*me, me, me!*"

We must move away from only seeking the *hand of God* and get back to seeking the *face of God*. This is, by definition, the *glory of God*.

"Show me Your face." That's what we should be saying. We are to seek the Kingdom of God first, and then all those other things will be added to us—but first things are first. Let's get back to seeking the Kingdom of God. The founder of the Salvation Army, William Booth, said:

> I consider that the chief dangers which confront the coming century will be religion without the Holy Ghost, Christianity without Christ, forgiveness without repentance, salvation without regeneration, politics without God, and Heaven without Hell.[4]

What needs to be addressed in the Church?

We have a Bible we don't read, a church we don't go to, and a Savior we don't make Lord. The challenge of today is not an unruly world, but an unaccountable Church.

A Bible We Don't Read

As I said earlier, a rightly divided Word will never produce a wrongly divided church. We get confused when we don't read the manual.

I built a swing set for our daughter Brooklyn when she was a child without reading the manual. I was proud of myself—until I got to the last piece and found out that I had put the first piece on backwards. I had to tear the whole thing down and start over. That time, I read the manual.

We need to abandon the professional church to go back to the primitive church. Otherwise, we're going to get to the top of a mountain and realize it's the wrong one. We must go back down the mountain we are climbing, pick up the guidebook, and find the right trail.

The Church must get back to the Word of God. It's the *will* of God, after all! We have to start reading the Bible. It is not an ancient book to prove religion true; it is the holy Word of God inspired by the Holy Spirit through man. It is a testament. A will.

When someone dies, they leave a testament or a will explaining how their property will be divided among their family members. The Bible contains all the promises that God has left to the believers on the earth. I am confident in saying this: If you fight the devil in your flesh, you will always lose, but if you fight the devil in the spirit, you will always win. The words of Jesus in your mouth are just as powerful as the Word in Jesus's mouth. It is so great that He said, "If you don't understand this parable, how will you understand any other parable?"

The Word of God is seed. The enemy comes in your life at two different times: when the seed is sown, and when the harvest is ready. The devil is not after you so much as he is after the seed of God inside you, which is the Word of God.

The Sower sows the word. God is so adamant about His words that He says He watches over them to perform them (Jeremiah 1:12); He says He has magnified His Word even above His name. His "word" refers to a promise.

Jesus once marveled at the faith of a centurion—a sinner— saying He had never seen such great faith. What did the centurion say to spark such a comment from Jesus? He said, "You don't have to come with me (to perform a miracle in person); I know that all you have to do is *speak a word!*"

The Word of God is still on the nation's bestseller list. Years ago, you could go into any hotel room and find a Bible in the nightstand drawer. Now the Word is on every phone and computer tablet and in the majority of bookstores and homes in our nation.

"Behold, the days are coming," says the LORD GOD,
"That I will send a famine on the land,
Not a famine of bread,
Nor a thirst for water,
But of hearing the words of the LORD." (Amos 8:11)

The Word of God is not inaccessible. It is available everywhere— but hearing, understanding, and fully obeying the Word of God is where we're experiencing a famine. Paul told Timothy that people one day would "have itching ears" and would "heap up for themselves teachers . . . and turn their ears away from the truth" (2 Timothy 4:3–4). That means we often want God to agree with *us* more than we want to agree with God. We must believe that the Word of God is the 100 percent infallible truth, and it's not to be changed or deconstructed. Psalm 119:89 says, "For ever, O LORD, thy word is settled in heaven" (KJV).

How will people hear without a preacher? That simply means the voice has to be strong in speaking the word of God. Don't think for a second that preaching follows mere ordination. No, preaching follows salvation. "Go into all the world and preach the Gospel." Don't go to listen; preach it. Evangelize it. Every single one of us is called to evangelize.

Righteousness, holiness, and godliness comes from our heart, not from following a list of rules. God never intended for us to have to strive to live godly lives. He said He wants people to follow Him because they *want* to, not because they *have* to—that's why He gave us free will. The only way the people are going to want to follow Him is through the Holy Spirit—so if I were the enemy, I would make sure no one experienced the true power of the Holy Spirit. Why? Because the Holy Spirit, by His definition in John 16, only agrees with the Words of God, the voice of God. There is no adaptation or addendum to the Word of the Lord; there are no loopholes. Many churches today are not rooted and grounded in the Word of God. We are feeding people spoonfuls of the world's sugar in an effort to make the medicine go down easier. We're not truly putting our knees on the ground and saying, "God, I'm yours." Strong churches result when people are rooted in the Word of God.

I encourage you to get back to reading the Word of the Lord. Give us this day our daily bread!

A Church We Don't Go To

The Church of Jesus Christ is not a building but a people. That means you're part of something public, not private. Nowhere in the Bible does it say anything about having church all by yourself.

"Church hurt" may be real. You may have had a bad experience. But eating bad chicken somewhere else has never stopped you from going to Chick-fil-A, bad service at a hotel doesn't make you stay home all the time, a wrong package from Amazon doesn't stop you from making another order, your car breaking down doesn't stop you from buying another one—and your mom or dad correcting you should not correlate with your finding another set of parents. One of today's challenges is the pervasive mindset among church members that everyone ought to be glad when they show up. But as the Book of Acts tells us, when the first church members didn't show up, they were the ones who missed out! We should have that mindset as well.

The Church of Jesus Christ is not a place, but a people. People today always ask *where* you go to church, but Jesus never defined the Church this way. It's not a what or a where, but a *who!* Paul emphatically said, "And let us not neglect our meeting together, as some people do, but encourage one another, especially now that the day of his return is drawing near" (Hebrews 10:25 NLT). I believe Paul saw something that would hinder the people of God from gathering in the last days. Think about that! Again, the early church grew without any social media, billboards, sound systems, smoke machines, or pipe organs. The building blocks of the Church were not sensory stimulation, but Spirit-filled living! Two things built the Church in Acts: Jesus Christ and the baptism of the Holy Spirit.

Jesus spoke those famous words to Peter, "Upon this rock I will build my church," when he was in the area of Caesarea Philippi, implying, "I'm going to build My church right in the middle of what you're seeing right now." At that moment, the inhabitants of Caesarea Philippi worshiped a Greek god named Pan, whose form was half goat and half human. Pan was often affiliated with sex, production, wildness, and springtime fertility.

Jesus was not saying He would build a church with sin. He was saying He was going to build a church right in the middle of sin and oppose it, causing people to turn to Him. The gates of hell were (and are) an actual place: a cave in Caesarea Philippi (modern-day Banias, Israel) believed to be the birthplace of Pan, so that's where the people of the area would go to worship him—often by human sacrifice. When people were thrown into that cave, a strong spring would gush from the earth and kill them. Jesus was looking at that place when He said, "Upon this rock I will build my church and the gates of hell will not prevail against it!"

Church, you are *called* out of this world—not taken out of this world immediately. If that wasn't the case, why did you not go straight to Heaven the moment you received Jesus Christ as your Lord and Savior? Because God has work for you to do here! He did not say He was going to take you out as soon as you got saved. No, Jesus actually prayed at the end of His life that the Holy Spirit would help us to govern the earth and be a mouthpiece for God. He did not call us to be worldly. He called us to go into the world…and then *preach!*

If you cannot physically speak, grab a pencil and start writing. If you can neither speak nor write, act it out. Whatever you do, don't stop being the voice of God on this earth. You cannot back down. You must raise your voice for righteousness and truth. The next generation is extremely confused about identity, God, Jesus, and when life begins, and are more concerned about being "woke" than being *wide awake*.

We are soldiers! We as the Church are called to separate. We are the "called out" ones. We are called to irritate Hell. We are the army of God. We're not on a cruise ship, we're on a battleship. Everything opposing you right now is also opposing the principles of God. An opposing force resents you for being the redeemed.

The Church is dreadful to the enemy, and the Church is militant. The Church has banners. The Church has authority, and the Church has power. There is nothing in existence like the Church of God filled and saturated with the Holy Spirit. No principality, ruler, or anything of the unseen world that opposes God's ways has the slightest power over the awesome might of His remnant. No principality, seen or unseen, can do anything with a house that is built on the name of the Lord Jesus Christ. The Church is a sacred house, a holy house; a house of which Jesus Himself is the cornerstone. Our children are going to be raised in the House of God, our marriages are consecrated by the House of God. That house, the Church, is built on the name of the Lord Jesus Christ. No other name carries the authority of Jesus Christ. Families are restored and demons are cast out by a Church that is called out. We are not brick and mortar. We are not chandeliers and light shows. We are not entertainment. We are not stages. We are the thriving, militant Body of Christ that sets the standard of God's righteousness in the nations.

The Church—the *ekklesia*, the *called out*—must become a family again. A place where people can belong and not just believe. The Bible calls us in Galatians 6:10 "a *household* of faith" (emphasis added). Our society is a reflection of the family. In order for the family to be repositioned to what God has called it to be, we must return to a noncompromising faith. "As for me and my house we will serve the LORD" (Joshua 24:15). Lines will have to be drawn not just over what we stand against, but what we stand for. God calls us a family. God is into family. He's the God of Abraham, Isaac, and Jacob. The Church must get back to caring for and honoring one another. You cannot truly participate in something you don't honor. The Church may disagree about some things, but don't all families disagree? Yet we still love one another—or at least, we should.

A Savior We Don't Make Lord

> If you confess with your mouth the Lord Jesus and believe in your heart that God has raised Him from the dead, you will be saved. (Romans 10:9)

This is a keynote scripture explaining how salvation works. Many people look at Jesus as only a savior, but this scripture has one word that changes everything: "lord." It is the word *kurios* in Greek and it means "absolute ownership rights." It also means "authority." Until Jesus Christ is lord over it, there will be a lack of authority in the Church, the Body. Many modern Christians believe that our confession is some kind of get-out-of-jail-free card, and we can keep on living the same way we did before we confessed Jesus. But that one word changes everything. It means that I no longer have my own rights, but I give up my rights and willfully submit my will to the Father. Salvation brought us out of the world, but until Jesus becomes lord over our fleshly desires, our need for acceptance, and our need to be understood, we will struggle.

This worldly system is no friend of ours. If we don't allow God to be the lord of our lives, we will continue agreeing with sin and soon find ourselves promoting and practicing it. We will store up worldly treasures in our hearts and conform to this world. But God called us to be transformed, to be completely different people governed by His Word and no other constitution.

Salvation carries a Moses anointing that brings you out of slavery with mighty blood over the doorposts of your life, but lordship carries a Joshua anointing that brings you into God's household with a fully obedient mindset that says, "What belongs to us belongs to *us!*"

Make Jesus lord and owner of your life, and become dead to the desire to live for yourself. *I am crucified with Christ, yet it is not I who live, but Christ in me.* We cannot be effective in this world unless Christ is in us.

CHAPTER 4

TICK-TOCK

The Clock Is Counting Down Every Day

Tick-tock! Get up! Get up! The Church is not asleep! That's what I heard from the Spirit of the Lord one morning before preaching in June 2022 as I descended into the lobby of a hotel in Houston, Texas.

I immediately had a vision. I saw a countdown clock, like the one you see at Cape Canaveral when a space shuttle is being launched. It was very large. All the hours and minutes had run out, and the clock was now counting off the final seconds.

I could not see the actual number, but I knew once it ticked away something was going to happen quickly. It was an event concerning America, and I believe it concerned the world as well. There was an urgency that made me feel we are in the eleventh hour.

I knew this was a vision sent by God because I could not shake it. What was about to happen? Was this the return of Jesus Christ?

Did the vision mean the Church is about to launch? Or maybe it was a warning that we are about to fall into captivity to another nation in ways we've never even imagined. I asked the Lord to send me to the Scriptures for an explanation. He immediately took me to Isaiah 1:9.

> Unless the LORD of hosts
> Had left to us a very small remnant,
> We would have become like Sodom,
> We would have been made like Gomorrah.

Even though it may seem like the world is overtaking the Church, there is a remnant!

When you see full-grown men and women changing their gender, when you see Satan being welcomed in after-school clubs or drag queens reading to our children in libraries and being embraced in the pulpits, you realize Satan is not hiding anymore. When you see people worshiping Satan as a god, you understand why they do the evil things they do. Many have no clue that they have fallen for a great deception. Satan knows his time is short.

If you are comfortable seeing what is happening in America and the nations right now, you are sitting at the wrong table. God said He would prepare a table *in front of* our enemies, not *with* them. While there are some things the Church does not celebrate openly, we *do* tolerate them. And whatever we tolerate, we will end up celebrating eventually. For example, 76 percent of those who call themselves evangelicals have agreed to and accepted the LGBTQ agenda. Like a Death Row inmate, we are being rendered unconscious before the chemical comes that stops our heart for good.

Pull out the needle of comfort and get on fire for God.

The world is being put to sleep by the enemy, but the Church is being awakened. The tick-tock sound may be soothing to babies, but it is irritating to adults. The clock on the wall can put people into a trance, but when a person is fully awake and resisting sleep, it aggravates him. Unless we are fully awake, we will not blow a trumpet; we will just watch what is going on. We must get up, *arise* and *shine*, for a light has come. Darkness is *covering* the landscape of the world. But God has a voice, a remnant!

Two Kinds of Clocks

Alarm clocks wake us up, but countdown clocks are different. While both are alarming, a countdown clock indicates finality. When an alarm clock goes off, someone is sleeping, but when a countdown clock is operating, people are wide awake and watching! COVID was an alarm clock. Now we're in the countdown.

Watching is not an activity that only engages our eyes. God does not hold us accountable for what we see happening that is out of our control. He holds us accountable for doing or not doing what we can in response to what we see going on around us. He told the prophet Ezekiel to blow the trumpet if he saw the enemy coming. He said if he saw them and did not blow the trumpet, He would regard their blood as being on his hands.

> [W]hen he sees the sword coming upon the land, if he
> blows the trumpet and warns the people, then who-
> ever hears the sound of the trumpet and does not take
> warning, if the sword comes and takes him away, his

blood shall be on his own head. He heard the sound of the trumpet, but did not take warning; his blood shall be upon himself. But he who takes warning will save his life. But if the watchman sees the sword coming and does not blow the trumpet, and the people are not warned, and the sword comes and takes any person from among them, he is taken away in his iniquity; but his blood I will require at the watchman's hand. (Ezekiel 33:3–6)

There is going to be a lot of blood on the hands of the redeemed because our eyes are "wide shut"!

The watchmen of the Bible were told to blow the trumpet to alert people who were sleeping; however, the watchmen themselves were not to sleep. A watchman must be *awake*, not woke, to what is happening or about to happen. He is to announce that somebody's coming and get everything ready for a fight. God also told Isaiah,

I have set watchman on your walls, O Jerusalem; They shall never hold their peace day or night. You who make mention of the LORD, do not keep silent. (Isaiah 62:6)

We are not called to be silent. That false humility is from the devil. Christians are supposed to be loud and impact the rest of the nation. We are to expose wickedness by raising our voice and speaking out. How will the sleeping wake up unless someone wakes them up?

Raise your voice!

The culture is loud. Satan is loud right now. However, I've seen the Church remain quiet on important issues out of fear. Our silence sings the loudest songs and preaches the loudest sermons. Neutrality is not an option. We have to find the will of God and the heart of God, even if many label it divisive. If you recall the parable of the wheat and the tares, the tares were sown while everybody was sleeping. It wasn't until everybody woke up that they realized there even were tares and began to speak about it. We must speak up, not just wake up!

The cancel culture of the past few years has caused many believers and many preachers to go quiet, supposedly for the sake of not offending others. Where does the Bible ever say we are not supposed to speak up? Where does it tell us to only say something if people want to hear it?

This countdown clock simply means there is no time left for us to sit and watch. We must stand and speak. We must refuse to be quiet in a world that is reeking of sin and accepting it.

Shaken and ready to blow the trumpet—that's the remnant right now. We do not accept that a church interior is the only place to voice our belief! No. We have been shaken, and we are under pressure. Just like a can of soda that has been shaken, the top needs to come off and the shaken Church needs to spew. The Church has been under pressure for too long to remain silent on so many issues—issues including racism, the destruction of the nuclear family, abortion, the LGBTQ agenda, the deconstruction of the Word of God, satanic agendas, gender reconstruction, pedophilia, and bestiality. We have seen the enemy coming for years and have not only failed to blow the trumpet, we haven't even taken it out of its case. Put the kazoo away and blow the trumpet! There should be a loud and resounding voice speaking out about the evils of our society. Time is short for change to come about. *Tick-tock!* There have to be preachers!

We are living in an unprecedented time. I'm not talking about the Church rising up, I'm talking about Satan's agenda rising up. He's not quiet, so why should we be quiet? We should go after this generation as hard as Satan does.

Revival happens because something is dead. I've never seen a dead man resurrect himself. Even Jesus did not raise Himself from the dead.

> But if the *Spirit of Him who raised Jesus from the dead* dwells in you, *He who raised Christ from the dead* will also give life to your mortal bodies through His Spirit who dwells in you. (Romans 8:11; emphasis added)

Therefore, our collective responsibility is neither individual awakening nor individual revival. Our responsibility is to *get up* after we've been awakened. This is where the Church must get it right. *We must get up.*

I'll say it again: We are not responsible to *wake up*, but we are responsible to *get up*.

The Church is not suffering from amnesia. We are suffering from anesthesia. We have been comfortably numb for too long. While I believe there is a powerful revival and awakening going on, we will have to continue to shake off our laziness and get to work. The Bible says "woe to [those] who are at ease in Zion" (Amos 6:1).

We can't confront sin if the Church is confused about what it is.

The Church looks like the world, and the world looks like the Church. As the Church goes, the nation goes. This is why it is imperative that we do not sit back and allow ourselves to remain numb.

Spiritual Anesthesia

We must not be numb. Anesthesia is given to avoid pain during an operation. Interestingly, there is one place in the body where a surgeon works that requires the patient to remain completely awake (and physically numb): the brain. God showed me this concerning the Church and how the enemy is working on us: He numbs you while you are awake so that you can see what is happening, yet he creates enough fear in you to do nothing about it!

There are three areas a brain surgeon takes special care not to damage—the ones controlling speech, vision, and movement. These are the three areas the enemy is hard at work trying to destroy in the Church.

Speech. Our speech is slurred with grace that condones rather than confronts. We speak little about the fear of God and more on the favor of God and favor of man. Because our speech is uncertain, the Bible says the people's blood will be on our hands. And I'm not talking about preachers only. I'm talking about every believer. I'm talking about *you*. I'm talking about *me*. *Your voice must not be random, but focused*. What you say impacts the gates of Hell. Don't allow your God-given authority to be diluted with fear or apathy. Speak up!

Vision. When you are comfortably numb, you can see what's going on, but you don't have the strength to address it. You can see hypocrisy, sin, and religion used as entertainment, but it doesn't affect you like it did when you were wide awake. Jesus told the luke-warm Laodicean church to buy eye salve so they could really see. He said, "You say 'I am rich, have become wealthy, and have need of nothing'—and do not know that you are wretched, miserable, poor, blind and naked" (Revelation 3:17). This Jesus we read about in the Bible is a different Jesus than we hear about in our churches right now. I firmly believe that the "Jesus" preached about and portrayed in mainline churches never would have been crucified. They make Jesus out to be weak and soft. However, He was very clear on sin.

Movement. The passivity of believers must come to an end. We are comfortably numb and going through the motions. We are hooked on stimulants rather than nourishment. We are hooked on hype rather than help. The enemy has numbed us into thinking that church is not church unless we are artificially moved. We must be stimulated through entertainment and stories of worldly antics to keep the church going. We make decisions to gather based on what songs a group sings, the screens they have, their light shows, and more. We have been conditioned to be entertained rather than to enter into the Presence of God. We have a church that twerks on Saturday and praises on Sunday—and is okay with that. As the old song says, we have grown "comfortably numb." We are not forcefully advancing, we are frolicking and playing *just enough* to make us feel good. In doing so, we are hindering the movement of God and grieving the Holy Spirit. Stop this passivity and soft, weak walk. We are to be bold as lions.

The longer you stay on anesthesia, the sicker you become. Even if the intention is good, it's still dangerous. We must recover from the slow, painless gospel. The struggle of the Gospel of Jesus should be welcomed even when it brings persecution, because Jesus said the persecuted would be blessed. In truth, it's a blessing to be able to feel pain. We must shake out of our comfortably numb state and raise our voice.

Tick-tock! There is a window of time left for the remnant to turn the Church's heart back to God. There will be multiple showdowns of epic proportion coming like the one between Elijah and the prophets of Baal which will prove God's authorities as well as His authority. The world saw Sam Smith and Kim Petras perform a song called "Unholy" with a full-on satanic worship ritual on stage at the 2023 Grammy Awards; three days later, revivals started breaking out nationwide in colleges and churches. These kinds of showdowns will continue to point God's people back to the wells of revival! He is going to back up His remnant. You must move now. You must see now. You must speak *now.*

If we do not, our silence will create captivity for our sons and daughters. Your children's children will be born into a society that looks completely different from the one you and I know. The Church must turn from our wicked ways. Note that 2 Chronicles 7:14 says, "If *my* people will…turn from their wicked ways" (emphasis added). This means you can be God's people and still have wicked ways. If we don't turn from them, time will run out and our children will eat the bread of our silence.

Time is short. Do an internet search for "Agenda 2030," and you will see that the United Nations has a plan for people, the planet, and prosperity. The World Economic Forum and other groups have similar plans. The world is setting itself up to have a single leader. You do not have to look far to see the call for politically uniting the world.

God prophetically spoke to me at the beginning of 2019. He said there is a "table of coexistence" being set at the holiest place on earth, Israel. What does that mean? At this moment, as I am writing this book, many people in Israel feel that they have found their Messiah. We have the Abraham Accords—a treaty President Trump brokered in 2020 normalizing diplomatic relations between Israel, the United Arab Emirates, Bahrain, Sudan, and Morocco—achieved in a mere five months. We have Muslims and Jews trying to achieve peace with each other, with a desire to bring Catholics, Protestants, Jews, and Muslims together to worship alongside each other. The Book of Revelation tells us this all transpires during the Great Tribulation. We are in the beginning of sorrows that Jesus spoke of in Matthew 24. While I don't want to date this book, the prophetic movements that we currently see on the world stage are extremely fateful. There has never been a better time in history for an outpouring of God's Spirit because there has never been a darker time in history.

The Next Inning

When I was growing up, my father had a picture in his office of a young boy playing outfield in a baseball game. There is a scoreboard in the distance that says "37–0." An old man leaning over the fence to talk to the young boy in the outfield says in the caption, "Don't you think you should quit?" The young boy's reply is priceless. "No, sir, our team hasn't been up to bat yet!"

This inning is nearly over, and the remnant believers are up next. Church, it is our turn. The enemy has delivered his best shot to take out the Church, to stop the gathering, and to silence the preaching of righteousness and holiness, but all of Heaven is standing at attention waiting on our next move. The alarm has gone off, and the countdown is ticking.

Your enemy was only promoted for a season to be embarrassed by the authority of the believer.

In Habakkuk, we learned that the Chaldeans were a bitter and hasty nation that were raised up to plunder the people of God. However, God tells the Israelites, "You're going to plunder what plundered you!" Romans 9 also tells us that God raised up Pharaoh for the purpose of displaying His own glory. Don't think for one second that time has already run out! Yes, time is running out, but you are the voice that can make time stand still! God heeded the voice of Joshua. God heeded the voice of Elijah. He told Samuel that not one of his words would fall to the ground. God loves it when we speak up on His behalf, especially when time is short.

You can't change what you won't challenge. Goliath taunted the Israelites day and night, and no one stepped up to the plate for forty days. Time was running out, and Goliath kept saying, "Give me a man that I can fight." I believe that's what the enemy has said to the Church. *Give me a man. Who's gonna step out and talk to me? Who's gonna fight me? I'm bigger than everybody.* Fear had paralyzed the people of God as Goliath challenged them, and the same thing is happening to us; we hear dire reports from news outlets first thing in the morning and before we go to bed at night. We are pumped with fear.

But David said, "I come to bring trouble back to you." While Goliath taunted him and said he was nothing but a stick, David raised his voice. *"You come to me with a spear and a sword, but I come to you in the name of the Lord!"* David should have said, "I come to you with a sling and a stone," but he was making it evident that he had a different weapon not made by human hands.

God is verifying and validating the voices that represent Him. Raise your voice now and fight from a different place. The weapons of our warfare are not carnal. They are mighty through God, *in prayer!*

It was a prayer meeting that started the whole revival in Acts 2. It was a prayer meeting that started the revival at Azusa Street in 1906. It was Jesus who said, "My house will be a house of prayer." Oh, that God's people would get back to the prayer meetings! The power of God flows through people who know how to pray. Don't just believe in prayer; believe there's power when you pray. The devil is paralyzed by praying people. Raise your voice in the prayer meetings; intercede on behalf of the next generation.

Tick-tock! The enemy is testing how far we will allow him to go. Just remember, *he can't do a thing without our consent.* This is what I have learned about how he works. Another thing I have learned about conditioning of the masses—whether by masks, stay-at-home protocols, vaccines, or anything else we may someday be forced to do—is that if you tell people the same thing long enough, they will believe it, even if it's a lie. They will first fear it, then consider it, then agree with it, then fear what will happen if they don't comply. In the end, the conditioned masses will tell others who aren't complying that *they* are the problem. Conform, or else.

Within the next few years, you are going to see the masses accept things they never would have accepted twenty years ago. All of it will look good, but hold fast to the word of the Lord! To five out of the seven churches of Asia Minor in the book of Revelation, Jesus said, "Hold fast." Paul also told Timothy, "Hold fast to the pattern of sound words which you have heard from me." This means that holding fast will be hard because bad people are raising their voices as well! But keep holding the Word as the authority. Do not allow those people to shape you; only allow the Word to shape you.

It Starts Now

I want to take things a step further. If you want to change a government, you often have to start in kindergarten. If you want to change Congress, start in kindergarten. If you want to change the White House, start in kindergarten. What is peddled to children in kindergarten is what they will accept, internalize, and propagate when they are adults. The enemy is after our children. *Tick-tock*. We only have a few years left. Say something for the sake of the children!

An opportunity closes as fast as it opens, just like a door that opens also shuts. While waiting has its place, right now is *not* the time for that. *We are not in a season to wait; we are in a season to war.* It's not a time to second-guess what's in your gut. The wilderness season is over, and it's time for battle. It's time to take ground. Don't allow deception to overtake you in this tick-tock season. If it is not rooted in the Word of the Lord, it's not the Lord. Question everything and hold it against the Word of God as the absolute authority.

Globalists with a new world agenda are taking aim, creating a false church that will rise up. It will look angelic, but it will be satanic! The one-world religion will sell you fear in the name of good.

This should not catch the believer off guard. Always remember, Satan has no power unless we give it to him. God calls each of us a king and a priest. The Bible says that Satan is the prince of the power of the air. A king always trumps a prince. Not only that, but

Jesus made sure He took every power away from Satan when He said on the cross, "It is finished." He disarmed him.

However, He did not take his voice away from him. Satan has no power, only influence—but he is great at it. If we're going to turn the tables as the Body of Christ and influence the world, we must be separated from it. The world is looking for answers right now, and the Church has them. *We have the answer, and we must herald the name of Jesus quickly. Time is short.* If we are not convinced that we have the answers, then the world will not be compelled to change anything. God needs you right now. *A revival of sanity and sanctification needs to happen in the sanctuary.* That means we must raise our voice and come out from the world.

We cannot continue to be mixed. Mixture is not good. Once a substance is mixed into flour, it takes sifting to remove it. Sifting is uncomfortable because the purpose is separation. This is what is happening in the Church right now. Even though it hurts, the end result is pure unity. Don't misunderstand the sifting as division; it's actually separation. It's simply removing what doesn't belong in the mixture. Righteousness cannot partner with wickedness. Light cannot live with darkness. What harmony can there be between Christ and the devil? How can a believer partner with an unbeliever? (2 Corinthians 6:14–18) Raise your voice!

There's nothing like the Church of God filled and saturated with the Holy Spirit. No principality or ruler can stand in the Church's away. The devil fears an awesome, powerful remnant of God. He cannot do anything with a house that is built on the name of the Lord Jesus.

And he knows it's tick-tock season. This is why wickedness is accelerating so quickly. It only makes sense for an enemy to attack when he knows his greatest threat lies just around the corner.

A lion roars for two reasons: to mark his territory and to warn of a threat. A lion will not roar if he is not threatened.

> Be sober, be vigilant; because your adversary the devil walks about like a roaring lion, seeking whom he may devour. (1 Peter 5:8)

A lion's roar can be heard up to five miles away. To a believer with authority, that doesn't mean the enemy is five miles away; it means, "I'm five miles away from taking what belongs to me." The Bible does not say that Satan is a lion, it says he is *as* a lion. He's a counterfeit. His roar is intimidation, but he can't stop a Church that roars back.

You belong to the actual Lion of the Tribe of Judah! Roar! Raise your voice. We must refuse to be intimidated by events, personalities, agendas, or entertainment that stifle God's ways! *Tick-tock*. He has given you His own authority to legislate on the earth; use it through prayer!

CHAPTER 5

CLEAN THE HOUSE

How God Is Preparing His Church in a Great Awakening

n 1946, Smith Wigglesworth said,

> When the new church phase is on the wane [decline]
> that would be the evidence in the churches of some-
> thing that has not been seen before. A coming together
> of those with an emphasis on the word and those with
> an emphasis on the spirit. When the word and the spirit
> come together, there will be the biggest move of the Holy
> Spirit that the nations and indeed the world has ever
> seen. It will mark the beginning of a revival that would
> eclipse anything that has ever been witnessed.[1]

Seventy-four years later, something terrible happened: COVID.

The year 2020 saw the greatest pandemic we have experienced in a century. COVID plagued the nations. No matter what you believe about it—whether it was man-made or came from somewhere else—it came. I lost my wonderful father to this pandemic. I'm still not sure if it was COVID or the medicine that took him out, but nonetheless, the pandemic initiated his final days.

Something felt off to me, though. Prophetically, it felt different; there was more to this than just a pandemic. There was a kind of reset and conditioning of the masses being initiated that would determine the course of the decade. Meanwhile, the global lockdowns had church leaders across the globe frustrated and challenged about how to keep their flocks gathering and their doors open. Would closing them show wisdom—or a lack of faith?

My wife and I pastor our church together, and I can tell you 2020 was one of the most challenging years of our lives. People would leave the church if you did not close the doors, and people would leave the church if you did close the doors. People would leave the church if you said to wear a mask, and people would leave the church if you said you didn't have to wear a mask. Nonetheless, most churches closed their doors and encouraged people to watch online through some type of livestream. Something spiritual was taking place. God spoke directly to my spirit, *COVID is not only a plague in the world, but also a purge in the Church.*

The 76 Percent Prophecy

I asked the Lord, "What is going on?" His response was very clear to me: "Wait for seventy-six."

I said, "Seventy-six?"

The Holy Spirit said, "When you see the number seventy-six, I will begin a work in My house and in My people."

My first thought was that's just not really a preacher-oriented thing to say. If God had said 75 percent, it would go with the parable of the sower, because Jesus taught that only 25 percent of the seed fell on good soil. Maybe it was seventy-five? But no. God said to release this prophetic word into the atmosphere everywhere I preach: "'When you see the number seventy-six, get ready, I'm going to do something,' says the Lord."

A few months later, in July 2020, the Barna Group released a report showing that 33 percent of church members were no longer watching online and did not plan to continue going to church.[2]

Wow! Within a few short months, 33 percent were gone. That didn't take long—but wait, it gets worse.

A few more months passed, and in March 2021, the Gallup organization released a report showing that for the first time in history, churchgoers had become the minority in America.[3] That made national news!

When the first Gallup poll on church attendance was conducted in 1937, 70 percent of Americans went to church. That number did not change significantly for decades. But because of COVID, less than half the population were faithful churchgoers.

Still, God continued to say, "Look for the seventy-six."

A short while later, another staggering report came out saying that 66 percent of former congregants would not be returning to church.

In April 2021, God sent me to the West Coast. At every stop along the way from San Diego to Los Angeles, I said that when we see the number 76, God would begin a move in His Church. It would mean something significant.

Shortly after I returned home to Georgia, the Associated Press published something that gave me goosebumps. It said: "Poll suggests 76 percent of Americans across most religions support LGBTQ equality."[4]

According to a poll conducted by the Public Religion Research Institute, 76 percent of the American church has embraced same-sex marriage. In less than eighteen months, the Church went from a majority to a minority, and even those who do consider themselves Christians are in favor of same-sex marriage. The whole time I prophetically heard, "seventy-six," I thought it had to do with church attendance—but it turned out church decline was connected to a deeper heart issue that had already gripped the Body: compromise!

God, what are You doing? I wondered. What a falling away! What a massive deception that has crept into the Church and surfaced during a pandemic—a time, you would think, when people would turn toward God. But no, 76 percent have turned away from truth and toward deception. They find church unnecessary and have moved God's boundaries on sexual matters. They claim that God is okay with sin because they are okay with it. The devil is very deceptive!

I recalled what Smith Wigglesworth said in 1946: "When the church phase is on the decline, get ready!" Well, here we are. The Bible clearly says in 2 Thessalonians 2 that before Jesus comes back, there will be a falling away. One of the greatest signs of the last seconds of the Last Days will be an apostate Church full of people who choose to ignore the Word of the Lord and leave the Body.

"Grace-only" preaching will result in lawless living, and this will lead to a lawless society that will in turn lead to the installation of a lawless leader called the Antichrist. In other words, it's not a lawless *world* that ushers in the end time, but a lawless *Church*. The world doesn't usher in apostasy; the Church does through weak and soft preaching. Soft preaching produces soft saints. It will take an apostolic authority to deal with an apostate Church.

Although I was discouraged to see the numbers plunge, I knew God was sending the purge, and it had to take place in order for something else to happen.

So, I asked, "God, what now?" and He said, "Go and see what happened in the upper room." And there it was.

First Corinthians 15:6 says that Jesus showed His resurrected body to five hundred people—but Acts 1:15 tells us there were only about 120 people waiting in the upper room on the Day of Pentecost. God told me to do the math.

500 − 380 = 120. The percentage of people left is exactly 76 percent of the original number.

That means 76 percent of those who saw the resurrected Jesus went back to their normal routines. I asked God, "What does this mean?" He said, *"I am cleaning the house like I cleaned the house in Acts."* What we see being purged is not just about what believers have accepted concerning the LGBTQ agenda, but other forms of unrighteousness as well—many more!

The Lord asked, "Why do you clean your house, Myles?" I knew exactly what He was saying. Sometimes, houses are in disarray. Maybe the carpets didn't get vacuumed, or the floors mopped; maybe the trash didn't get taken out; the dishes were left undone, or there was clutter that needed to be removed because we had been busy and felt we had no time. But one thing always motivates us to get the house in order and cleaned, swept and ready: when we hear that *company is coming.*

The power of the Holy Spirit did not fall upon the five hundred, but it did fall upon the 120. *Exactly* 76 percent of the people left before the company came. What a staggering coincidence that what we have experienced during and after COVID is what occurred fifty days after Jesus was crucified: *Pentecost.* Can you imagine if you were one of the people in the upper room, but you got hungry or tired of waiting and went home—and ten minutes later there was the sound of a rushing wind, and everyone began speaking in tongues and prophesying while flames of fire appeared over their heads? What if you heard that sound, turned around, and saw the fire of God fall on each of the people who stayed in the room—but you missed it? What a miserable feeling that would be, knowing that you left too soon.

It is evident that God is beginning to visit His people in an extraordinary way. Multiple college campuses and churches, both in our nation and elsewhere, are seeing the wells of revival open up, similar to the Book of Acts, in 2023. Get ready, because the Church is beginning to look different. I believe that your services, your streets, and your homes will be completely overwhelmed by the penetrating power of the Holy Spirit. Prepare for services to last longer than one hour and fifteen minutes. Make room for miracles to break out, for blind eyes to open, and for demons to be cast out and sickbeds to be brought in. People will be healed. Get yourself in position for God to use you. The Holy Spirit is coming with a fresh wind upon His Church.

Shaking, Shifting, Sifting, Gathering

When I talk about cleaning house, I'm talking about the House of God. When 76 percent of people can embrace homosexuality as normal, it's a sign that the righteous judgment of God is going to fall. We have people who call themselves "reverends" who openly march in gay pride parades. We have megapastors partnering with leaders of other religions at the table of coexistence, mingling Abba with Allah as if they're the same person. We have churches that have become political hubs, and we have preachers who feel it's okay to promote abortion, as if God is okay with this. It's amazing to me how easy it has been for compromised preachers to raise their voice to say what people want to hear.

But when it comes to the sticky things, the things that God speaks about? Then we hear nothing but crickets. I was appalled by the silence from the churches when the U.S. Supreme Court overturned *Roe v. Wade*. I was expecting social media to blow up with megapreachers and Spirit-filled churches praising the fact that a practice that has killed sixty-two million children in the womb is no longer a federal issue, but something for the states to decide for themselves. What an incredible moment in our nation's history! And yet, so many large ministries said nothing! Why? Were they afraid to offend people—that it might cost them people in their pews or coins in their coffers? That's a problem with Christians today: we are offended so easily. What about that which offends God?

God is the One who gives us our platforms, our ministries, our finances, our buildings, and our opportunities to preach. I will tell you why God has shaken and continues to shake and clean the house: because the trash has piled up so deeply that it's making the whole house stink. He is scraping the leaven off the walls, purging the secret sins, and exposing the fake grace and lawless living in His house. God help the preachers who have preached false doctrine, those who have embraced sin and condoned it from the pulpit!

God is shaking, shifting, sifting, and gathering. It is going to happen quickly! Prepare yourself to be a voice in this season and to speak on behalf of God. I believe that's why you are reading this book. The Spirit of God is going to jump off these pages and give you a boldness to call people back to a standard of righteousness, graced by holiness, godliness, and Spirit-filled living.

Shaking

God woke me up with a prophetic word on September 27, 2020, at 6:30 a.m. He said,

"The standard is being raised. It's a banner! I have released voices on the earth today that will not flirt with foolishness or cower to speak. For I, the Lord, am to be feared and revered, and I, the Lord, will shake the people—and I will shake with vengeance. I will shake with vengeance to align My people to My will, and I will cause Heaven's provision to fulfill my purpose. Supernatural favor will belong to the people of God. Speak, and speak loudly! The favor of God is unleashed upon those who raise their voices and speak. I will deliver My glory to those who are prepared for Me. I will not battle with Babylon, but I will snuff wickedness out. I will increase favor upon My people, and I will render Heaven's storehouse open for My glory to be fully funded on Earth. You will see My glory—and no man can stand in My glory and not change, no woman can stand in My glory and not be fruitful, for

I, the Lord, speak, and My glory shows up like a fire. Torches are lit, light it up! For I am sending you into the camp just as Samson sent the foxes into the camp of the Philistines, two by two, tied together. Did I not light the tails? Did I not light the tails on fire? So shall I light you. I would like you to burn the harvest of your enemy, and I will light your tails on fire! You will not be able to sit down, you will not be able to sit still until the harvest of your enemy is fully on fire. I, the Lord, am changing the frequency and you will hear clearly divine direction."

That word to me was confirmed by Scripture:

> "Yet once more I shake not only the earth, but also heaven." Now this, "Yet once more," indicates the removal of those things that are being shaken, as of things that are made, that the things which cannot be shaken may remain. Therefore, since we are receiving a kingdom which cannot be shaken, let us have grace, by which we may serve God acceptably with reverence and godly fear. (Hebrews 12:26–28)

The year 2020 brought a great shaking. Notice that Hebrews says when God shakes something, two things happen: all that can be shaken is removed, and all the things and people that could not be shaken are revealed. That means if you're still here and resolute about the things of God, you *remain*. You are part of the remnant.

The purpose of the shaking is not to focus on who left, but who *is* left! While the statistics seem bad, the truth is that God has been cleaning the house to purify the voice of the remnant. The shaking was *necessary*. The shaking season reveals which kingdom you are a part of.

> Therefore, since we are receiving a kingdom that cannot be shaken, let us have grace, by which we may serve God acceptably with reverence and godly fear. (Hebrews 12:28)

The shaking took out people who did not serve God with reverence and godly fear. I believe the fear of man had replaced the fear of God in many. When you walk in the fear of God, you'll speak up for Him even when persecution comes. God has given us many opportunities to put our faith and trust in Him, yet the fear of man caused many people to stumble. Doctors, political leaders, and media outlets turned our hearts of faith into hearts that feared.

Everybody says they want an awakening, but a *great shaking happens before a great awakening.* Whether you believe it or not, the great awakening is upon us. It has been a rude awakening.

When you wake up in the middle of the night, you're simply not coherent for a second. You have to gather your thoughts, take inventory of where you are, and shake yourself out of a slumber. I once woke up at 3:00 a.m. to an alarm at my house. I grabbed my gun and swung it around the room while my wife screamed, "Don't shoot, don't shoot!" I was not coherent, but I was ready to fight. However, because I had just been awakened by the alarm, I was still confused about *what* to fight. That's what I believe has happened to the Church. *We know an alarm has gone off, and we know there is an awakening, but we're still confused about what we should raise our voice to speak about.*

We have been so inundated with numb living that when we are jolted awake, we have a hard time responding. The shaking is to jolt us. The Church cries out for an awakening, and then God sends one—because something is asleep.

Now that you're awake, not woke, it's time for the second part of cleaning the house: the *shift!*

Shifting

A shift entails a changing of the guard. God is calling those who could not be shaken to begin to shift out of the old season and into the new one. God does not put old wine into new wineskins. A new sacrifice has to be made for a new wineskin; they go hand in hand. That means that God continues to clean His house to get rid of ways that are not working and agendas that are not anointed. This is the exit season from the old ministry. The recent outpourings of God's presence at Asbury and other college campuses and churches are indicators of a season changing. God's wind is blowing in a fresh way, and we must be careful not to stay with old wineskins that are familiar to us. You cannot continue to mechanically attend church and believe that you're living for God. God has taken you off of autopilot. This season is not an automatic shift, but a manual shift.

When I was growing up, my father taught me how to drive a stick shift car. It requires you to be hands-on. You can't just put it in drive; you have to continually work the gears. With your left foot, you push the clutch pedal down while your right hand works the gear shift. You have to shift when you reach the maximum revolutions per minute for that gear. If you keep the car in first gear, the automobile will get loud but never able to reach full speed and power. The power of the engine has already been set, but in order for you to maximize it, you have to shift from one gear to the next.

The shifting season cleans the house because it demands you get back to putting your foot down and being "hands on." You can no longer sit in the audience or on the sidelines and just let the gears turn automatically; you are called to participate. That's always been our role in the Kingdom of Heaven. When we lose sight of it, God calls us into a shaking and a shifting. The Kingdom of Heaven is never about observation, but participation. In other words, you can't just sit quietly. The Kingdom of Heaven moves through your participation.

Put your foot down. Put your hands on the lever, and shift. In this next season, you're not allowed to sit quietly. Your voice has to activate others, and that means you have to move from being concerned to being consumed. When God shifts a people, He stirs them up and requires them to walk by faith. No more crying about what is gone. No, a new voice is rising up to shift not only you, but an entire nation, to get up and speak up. Raise your voice!

Sifting

This is the part of cleaning the house where God begins to separate. The voices of the last season who refused to stand up when it mattered are currently being sifted. God is not playing around. It's revival or resignation! His servants must step up to preach against sin and raise up the standard of holiness. A showdown is coming between good and evil, and God is looking for some Elijahs who don't mind being set apart. When you operate this way, many people will say you're being divisive—but don't confuse division with separation. Sifting is simply separating.

Why do we have to be sifted? Because there has been too much mixture. Mixture is killing the Church and confusing the next generation. Mixture creates dullness of hearing. Hearing and speaking go together. Naturally, when someone cannot hear well, it also creates a speech impediment. So, in order to speak well, you must hear well. Jesus said in Matthew 24 that lawlessness would abound and the love of many would grow cold, but he who endures to the end shall be saved. Endurance simply means there is a day coming when it will be hard to preach the Gospel because of the delusion and deception that is so rampant on the earth. Good and evil will seem identical, and people will embrace perversion but call it holy. This happens because of spiritual immaturity. Our voice for God becomes unrecognizable when the hearing of the Word has been tampered with.

> You have become *dull of hearing.* For though by this time you ought to be teachers, you need someone to teach you again the first principles of the oracles of God; and you have come to need milk and not solid food. For everyone who partakes only of milk is unskilled in the word of righteousness, for he is a babe. But solid food belongs to those who are of full age, that is, those who by reason of use *have their senses exercised to discern both good and evil.* (Hebrews 5:11–14; emphasis added)

We are dull of hearing because we have not exercised our ability to distinguish both good and evil. You have to know both. For twenty years, we've really heard about the good, but we have not developed our ability to differentiate the evil. The word "discern" is *diakrisis*. It means to have a proper judgment and ability to distinguish between lookalikes that appear to be the same. We have to regularly exercise our ability to discern.

Many times, I have met twins I could not tell apart. They looked alike to me, even though they're separate people. It wasn't until I spent time with them that I could see the minor differences between them—birthmarks, personalities, emotions, expressions, and ways they communicated. If you talk to the twins' parents, they could tell you exactly who each twin is because they created them. They gave them their identities. They gave them their names. The parents had no problem with mixing up their children, but others had to learn to see the differences between them by spending time with them.

We tend to think that God's words and the enemy's words sound different, but that's not true. From the beginning of time, we've found that one of Satan's greatest weapons is twisting God's words. Satan has always used the Word of God. I love what A. W. Tozer says: "The devil is a better theologian than any of us and is *a devil still*" (emphasis added). The devil manipulated Eve with the words of God. When he tempted Jesus, he used the words of God. But Jesus didn't fight Satan with a song or with emotions. He didn't hope to get to church on Sunday so that someone else could take care of the devil. No! In power and authority, He *raised His voice* to Satan and told him what the written Word of God says. That is what we need to do. We need to hit the talk-back button and hit him with the Word of the Lord.

And no wonder! For Satan himself transforms himself into an angel of light. Therefore it is no great thing if

his ministers also transform themselves into ministers
of righteousness, whose end will be according to their
works. (2 Corinthians 11:14–15)

Satan will allow his ministers to preach either the law or the
Spirit separately, but the law as established by faith in Christ's righteousness and atonement, as well as the partaking of His Spirit, is
the test of every false system. We shouldn't expect Satan to appear
to man to be as bad as he is in reality. He never shows himself
openly to be a spirit of pure wickedness, black and abominable in
his character, or full of evil and hate. He would defeat himself this
way. Instead, he will say things like "love your neighbor"—but in
an inappropriate context. I believe that in the last days, the mark of
the beast will be accepted because it will be given to us "out of fear
in the name of good." If we are not separated from the world, if we
haven't removed the mixture within us, we will be deceived. Our
enemy is devious, and he will appear to be good in order to conquer
us from within the walls of the Church. *No outside persecution or
force ever crushed the Church; rather it caused it to grow. It is the
inside mixture that causes the Church to either remain stagnant
or decline.*

Just before the greatest gathering of all time happens, the
Second Coming of the Lord, there will be an amazing deception.
Jesus told us in Matthew 24 what to look for and then followed up
with parables to help us understand what it would look like. We
spend a lot of time looking for Him, but not enough time understanding what things will look like before He comes back.

The parable of the ten virgins illustrates this: Five wise and five
foolish virgins awaited the return of their master at night, but only

half of them brought extra oil; the rest ran out. The first thing that stands out to me is that while the Church is being sifted and separated, we'll look very much alike. All ten virgins took their lamps and torches. All ten went out to meet the bridegroom—and all ten slumbered. (That tells you why the Church needs the awakening just as badly as the world! Even the five wise virgins were sleeping!) Then the awakening call came, and all ten virgins awakened. All ten virgins trimmed their lamps, but five had no oil. Oil is the only thing that separates them; the five foolish ones ran out of the ability to discern good and evil.

The awakening call came at midnight. That tells you that when the Lord Jesus comes back, it will be at the darkest hour. There will be such a lawlessness in the last days that the awakening will shock people. Still, only half of those who have a light will make it. Light represents knowledge. Discernment comes from knowledge. Amos 8 says that people are destroyed because of their lack of knowledge. Also, don't sell your oil. Never sell out! When God comes to clean the house, make sure the oil stays with you. That last bit of oil is what makes all the difference!

What a tragedy to run out of oil. The lamps didn't rescue the virgins, it was the oil. God calls us "the light of the world" not "the oil of the world." Oil is something that is produced within us by the Holy Spirit. You cannot produce the oil in your own strength.

This is why it is so necessary to understand mixture. The Bible says we are not to allow any folly to mix with the anointing (Ecclesiastes 10:1). It's God's precious oil. When you understand mixture, you will see that entertainment and entering God's Presence are two different things when it comes to worship. We have to know how to be different in order to speak differently. Our adulterated lifestyle as Christians calls us to preach grace without truth.

It's sad to say, but most people who focus on preaching only the grace of God are often the ones who need it the most. You have to preach 50 percent grace and 50 percent truth to preach the 100 percent Gospel. Since many have a mixture of sin with their salvation and conclude that God is okay with this state of things, they become silent on issues that involve them. Our silence on sin sings the loudest songs and preaches the loudest sermons.

Sifting gives you the ability to see between the real and the fake. I once was on the set of a major television network; there was a beautiful fireplace in the background. The fire was burning brightly, and everything was set for an incredible night of interviews. When it was my turn to be invited onto the stage, I realized there was no warmth coming from the fire. It was just paper strips being moved back and forth by a fan, with red and orange lights shining on them. The whole time I was looking at the fireplace from a distance, it looked real. It wasn't until I got close to it that I realized: *This is not fresh fire. This is* fake *fire.*

This really seems like where we are.

This reminded me of the scripture in 2 Timothy 3:5 that says people will have a form of godliness, but they will deny its true power. They will look like they are godly, but they're not going to have any oil. They're going to look like they have fire, but there won't be any warmth or heat coming from them.

The grace of God confronts; it doesn't condone. A true altar has the fire of God on it. We must learn how to differentiate real flames from fake fire. To do so, we have to separate ourselves from the fake fire. The only way to do that is to get close to God and disassociate with anything that doesn't come from Him. When you go through the sifting, you will distinguish the difference between fake fire and fresh fire.

Jesus spoke about the lukewarm church of Laodicea in Revelation; because it was neither hot nor cold, He would vomit it out of His mouth. Historians tell us the city of Laodicea had three different streams of water running through it: a stream of hot water, a stream of cold water, and a stream of lukewarm water. The hot and the cold water were usable because they were pure. However, the lukewarm water had contaminants in it, a mixture. Anytime anyone drank it, this water would make them sick.

Once, when I visited the Bahamas, my parents told me not to drink the water because my system couldn't handle the contaminants in it. I was careful to drink only bottled water. However, when I went to get ice cream, I didn't realize the ice cream scoop was being washed with local water. Man, did I enjoy that ice cream—until the middle of the night, when I woke up and started throwing up everywhere. The contaminated water got into my system, and then a natural progression took place, leading to my body throwing up the contaminants.

Here's the challenge: If I were to move to the Bahamas, I would become accustomed to drinking the water, and my system would eventually be okay with it. That's how we are with sin. If we don't continue to stay separated as a people, we will conform rather than be transformed. Our voice will become diluted with outside contaminants and mixture—and Jesus is coming back for a spotless Bride, without blemish or wrinkle (see Ephesians 5:27). Before there is a gathering, God will always clean the house through sifting.

Gathering

Have you noticed what has been attacked over the last few years? It's been the gathering of the believers! The devil is not afraid of a church building, he's afraid of the Church gathering. *Satan only attacks where he knows there is a threat.* The enemy is well aware of what happens when we get together in unity.

What do I see happening in this season? A great gathering of Holy Ghost-filled, remnant people who will meet together at any cost. God help us with the gathering! If all we have left are 120 people who don't represent the majority, so be it. I am not after division; I am after separation. Those who are called and separated are beginning to gather. We are seeing the greatest move of God the world has ever seen. Voices: gather now.

I am encouraging you right now to prepare your heart for God to fill you with His powerful and precious Holy Spirit. *Company is coming! Another great outpouring of the Holy Spirit is here.* I remember the Lord telling me, "Before Jesus comes back *to* the Church, He's going to come *through* the Church." John the Baptist said Jesus has a winnowing fork in his hand, and He is going to thoroughly purge.

What happened in Acts is happening today. There is a new, fresh empowerment of the Holy Spirit pouring out to you and others who have stayed—to pour out like it's never poured out before.

Listen: The Holy Spirit can be *around* you, and you will feel the presence of God. The Holy Spirit can come *upon* you, and you will have an unction to do specific and supernatural tasks. But when the Holy Spirit gets *in* you, watch out! Because the first thing you will do is start raising your voice. You will become a voice that irritates

Hell and brings Heaven down. Your mouth becomes a trumpet for the Lord, and you begin to speak with authority. The devil cannot do anything with somebody under the power of the Holy Spirit. You won't tiptoe around the kingdom of darkness, but you will lift up your voice and speak straight into it.

Oh, how we need preachers filled with the Holy Spirit, speaking for the Lord, raising their voices just like Peter raised his. He told the people what they were doing was wrong, but he also told them how to do right—and the people were cut to the heart (Acts 2:37). The next thing you see is people giving their hearts to God by the thousands, praising God and receiving favor.

As promised, on the other side of this purge is an outpouring of the Holy Ghost. The same thing that happened in Acts is happening today. God has cleaned the house on purpose. Keep digging those wells, going after God, and separating from the world.

Church is beginning to look different. The gap between the pulpit and pews is diminishing. Worship is changing, and the congregations are not watching worship anymore. They are worshiping. I believe that our services, our streets, and our homes will be completely overwhelmed by the penetrating power of the Holy Spirit. Because of the hunger of the people, services are lasting longer than one hour and fifteen minutes. This is the season where miracles are breaking out; blind eyes will open and demons will be cast out, sick beds will be brought in, and people will be healed. Get yourself in position for God to use you. *Company has come!* The Holy Spirit is moving in the hearts of believers everywhere, and a great outpouring is upon us. Lay hold of this moment, raise your voice with righteousness, and turn the hearts of the people back to God.

CHAPTER 6

EMERGENT DIVERGENT

A Critical Mass Is Forming, and They Look Different!

How will we see Kingdom unity without being separated by a critical-mass incident in the Church? We could call it the United States of a Divided Church. I watched a movie a few years ago called *Divergent*. When the storyline started to unfold, I realized this is exactly what the Lord has been doing with a small faction of people inside large groups: divergence!

In this movie, the world has supposedly been destroyed, and an elite group of people has built their own utopia and set up boundaries to keep the survivors quarantined from the outside world. After years of developing their political system and way of life, the new society has been divided into factions. When children grow up, they are to choose a faction, even if doesn't fit their bloodline. The five factions are:

1. ERUDITE: The intelligent, scholastically inclined, philosophical people who search for truth
2. AMITY: The peaceful, simple-minded people who seek harmony above all else
3. CANDOR: Those who value honesty and order above all else; truth-tellers and interpreters of the law
4. DAUNTLESS: The brave and "free" people who serve as soldiers and police
5. ABNEGATION: The selfless; helpers who deny themselves

Between these factions, and these factions only, did the society remain balanced. Anything else was considered a threat—particularly those individuals called "divergent," who displayed multiple characteristics of the other factions, rather than fitting neatly into just one mold. The word simply means *different*—but the divergent were frowned upon, and more importantly, they were targeted by the society's elite leaders.

But the divergent didn't know they were different than the others until they took a series of tests. Once they did, everything began to make sense to the divergent because they were able to see beyond the societal boundaries that had been created.

While the tests were designed to classify people and make them fit in, they showed the divergent that they would never fit in and that the social elites would never control them.

In the movie, they were called "divergent"; in God's house, they are called "the remnant."

I am fully convinced that God has raised up—and is raising up—an army of fiery voices. These people are tested by the Word of God and refined by His holy fire. They are not molded by current cultural trends but are tempered by the hand of God. Maybe you are one of those divergent voices. A group of wilderness waiters, not wanderers; being formed on the backside of the desert while also being called on to the frontline of God's army! When these people speak, they don't sound like normal, everyday preachers. They are not passive or political. They are powerfully *different* voices, often misunderstood. These people look like everyone else, but they don't think, act, or sound like everyone else. They are *divergent*.

Divergents have no fear of man, but they are very reverent of God. They are those who live a "whatever He says" way of life. You can't control them through factions. They are completely surrendered to God. God has them in His quiver, and He is launching His arrows in this new season. The *Voice of God* speaks through these divergents. They are out of step with the world. Don't get me wrong, they know order; they know respect for authority, and they know honor, but they hear a different drumbeat. It is possible that the factioned church will push away these voices that emerge at first, but the divergent will not cease to demand change for God. A revolt may be necessary to bring true and lasting freedom from tyranny to God's people.

You may feel as if you don't fit. The current culture will label you a defect, but God is raising you up as a deliverer. Divergent people have I-don't-fit personalities.

Not only do divergent people not fit in—they may feel as if they are not necessary. Nothing could be further from the truth! They are clearly a remnant. When you come to the end of a roll while laying carpet, there is a piece that is not used because it just doesn't fit! They call this a "remnant." This silent yet numbing inner voice tells you that you aren't necessary. You must silence that thought quickly before it takes root, because it comes from your enemy. People want you to fit into the mold, do what they do, and speak the way they speak. This is the complete opposite of an emergent divergent. Raise your voice and swim upstream! You will never fit in!

Moses is a prime example of a divergent. Moses didn't ask to be born, but God needed a voice that would not only decree but deliver. Even his name means "draw out," and that is what he did for the people of God. He never fit in. When Moses was born, Pharaoh had already issued a decree to kill the Israelites' male children in order to keep them from becoming more numerous than the Egyptians and thus overthrow the people who enslaved them. All the boy babies had to be tossed into the river!

It's amazing to me that Moses was drawn out of water and a pharaoh was killed in water. While one pharaoh ordered babies to be killed in the river, the next pharaoh was executed by God in the Red Sea!

Wow! Think about that through the lens of Providence. God has a way of using your enemy's weapons against him: Esther's husband hung Haman on his own gallows. David stunned Goliath with a stone, but he killed him with his own sword. The ironic truth is that the greatest weapons formed to take you out inevitably are what God uses to wield the greatest victories in your life! Moses did not fit in. He was a Hebrew man in the system of Pharoah. Even while he was considered an insider of insiders—part of the king's court—he couldn't fit in. But he wasn't a slave, so he also didn't fit the Hebrews' social conditions. He was in the world's system, yet he couldn't stand to see God's people kept in bondage. He was a caged deliverer. *His voice was locked up by the cultural norms of his day.* He felt the need to step in and stop the oppression, but when he did, the people of Israel—his own people—turned on him. *When you are a voice for God, you will have to navigate all types of misunderstandings.*

The children of Israel wanted freedom, but not at the price freedom would demand. *They needed someone to go before them!* Wow. That is a tough place for Moses to be. The world was trying to kill him, and the Hebrews wouldn't accept him. When you are an emergent divergent, stop looking for the people to agree with you. That may never happen. Radical preachers and revivalists typically don't get invited back to preach at many churches. Why? Because they are not wanted until they are needed! What they say seems offensive because it crosses the overly cute church norms that we have slowly adopted. A divergent voice doesn't sound like freedom at first; it sounds like sandpaper. A voice of fire never feels inviting, but it is crucial for getting people into the next season.

It doesn't matter what decrees have been made to kill you. When you are a divergent, you continue to obey the call of God on your life even when you are met by spiritual snipers and are out of step with the rest of the group. Enduring this testing in your life confirms that you were born not only to be free, but to free everyone in bondage. The emergent divergent hate bondage on any level, whether in the world or the Church—bondage which is often referred to as religion. Relevance is not what the emergent divergent are looking for, but revival for the people.

They are already on the earth. The Bible says that before the people cried out for a deliverer, Moses had already been born. God raises a crier before people cry out—a preacher, a voice, a divergent. Our crying out for a revival and for God to move on the earth is an indication that He already has deliverers here. God is proactive. He's already got someone in the wilderness ready to raise his voice and bring freedom.

The divergents will look like you, but when they come, they won't sound like you. They have been through difficulties. They were not born to stay in a situation that God has called them to bring people out of. The Voice of God goes forth from the emergent divergent with vengeance. I am asking you reading this to make room for that inner voice in your life and allow God to test the religious, invisible boundaries that the society elites of the Church have set. The voice of God is going to free you in areas you didn't even know you were experiencing bondage.

The test is to prove *you* faithful, not to prove that God is.

Psalm 105:16–22 says,

> Moreover He called for a famine in the land;
> He destroyed all the provision of bread.
> He sent a man before them—
> Joseph—who was sold as a slave.
> They hurt his feet with fetters,
> He was laid in irons.
> Until the time that his word came to pass,
> The word of the LORD tested him.
> The king sent and released him,
> The ruler of the people let him go free.
> He made him lord of his house,
> And ruler of all his possessions,
> To bind his princes at his pleasure,
> And teach his elders wisdom.

Joseph was deeply misunderstood at the beginning of his life. After he revealed the dreams God gave him about his destiny, his family was the first to hate him. All Joseph had was the promise of a dream that God had given him. In order to get to the provision, he would have to go through major testing. Psalm 23 tells us there is a place where we shall not want, where there are green pastures and still waters! Then there is a place where the cup is running over, our enemies are made to watch us eat the fruits of our successes, and goodness and mercy follow us. But what about that middle part—walking through the valley? The shadow of death? That doesn't seem to fit the psalm. Promise and provision, remember? But between the promise and the provision are problems. The test. God works this way in our lives.

JUST ENOUGH = still waters

NOT ENOUGH = trust God in the valley

MORE THAN ENOUGH = cup overflows

Most people are satisfied with "just enough," so they never get to a divergent mindset. They are happy to stay in the rationing of religion. But the test is in the valley. It causes you to see the Word in a different light and to open your eyes to the world around you and how you can effectively free others from their bondage. The test is for promotion. We taste to see how God is faithful to us; God tests to see how faithful we are to Him.

Critical Mass

Critical mass is the size that something needs to reach before a particular change, event, or development can happen. For example, if you go to midtown Manhattan, you will see people waiting at the corners for the "walk" sign to come on before they cross the street—but if enough people gather, the crowd will spill into the street even before the light changes, and the whole group will cross against traffic. The pedestrians overtake the flow of the traffic because they reach critical mass.

It only takes a fraction to change the factions. Five percent of the church in America today is roughly equal to 1.6 to 2 million people. Once a group grows to 2.5 to 5 percent, it begins to change the composition of the whole.

If you don't know what to do about the compromise you are seeing in the Church, the answer is to gather the emergent divergent and begin to wait on the Lord together. It's going to look like an "upper room" experience. Can you imagine 1.6 million people in America being baptized in the Holy Spirit? Dream for a minute with me. We would turn the world upside down!

> "These men who have turned the world upside down
> have come here too." (Acts 17:6 AMP)

Why "emergent" divergent? Emergent means arising and quickly coming forth; a quick separation of those God has called out of the silence and shadows to the forefront. They have been hidden for such a time as this. There will always be separation that comes from agitation before God brings unification. The emergent divergent are separating quickly for the cause of a powerful revival of unity that will take place.

The Church has been subpar for way too long. Our desire for unity is met with resistance. It seems we cannot set aside our titles, political persuasions, or religious affiliations long enough to unify.

Even the color of our skin gets in the way of real change. It feels as if there are fifty-two thousand denominations in America alone. We need unity. Not at the price of universal thinking or acceptance and tolerance of sin, but rather with the central focus of the critical mass being *Jesus Christ*. God is not looking for soft speakers or relevant rhetoric. He is looking for demonstration!

We can no longer just discuss what needs deliverance in our nation. Casting out a demon doesn't happen through discussion. No, it happens through the use of authority. The demoralization of men and women, the redefinition of nuclear family, the legalization of sin, and the racism that exists around the entire color wheel demand that we rise up with *bold authority* and cast it all out. A new norm must come into Christianity, which will then become a force among the nations. We want change? At what cost? It will rock the little kingdoms that we have built—but rock them for a greater cause. We must seek towels over titles and serving over being served. We must combine radical love with a radical perspective of God's people. The need is too great. We must bring unity to God's people now—not only for our sakes, but for our children and for our nation.

There is a riptide churning the waters of church culture. You can't see a riptide when you're in the water; the only way to see it is to get to a higher level. This is why lifeguard stands are raised to a higher altitude. The Latin word *altus*, meaning "high," is where we get both the words "altitude" and "altar." Altars are always found in high places. So to see the riptides brewing in the church culture is to get to the altar together. Riptides are dangerous because they don't form during a storm; they typically form on clear days right after storms, when it looks like it's safe to go to the beach. I see so many people in church lose their grounding in what church is actually about, putting the social aspects of it over salvation, getting caught in the riptides of religion and formalities to the point that it only takes a little while and a little mixture provided by the religious elite to pull them off the stable shore and out into the deep waters of division.

Satan's kingdom has no power, but it is extremely organized. The Church has all power but is extremely disorganized. Satan's plan is to keep us ineffective for any real change to our nations concerning righteousness. Therefore, we must unite the emergent divergent voices in this nation to see *real change*.

About Racism

The emergent divergent is a group of all colors of people! All hues. Racism is killing the Church. We are not here to compete with each other, but to complete each other. We are not here to overpower one another, but to empower one another. We are not here to be served, but to serve. Racism is more than just a *skin* thing; it's a *sin* thing! Our races may be different, but our righteousness comes from the same Source: Jesus. Unity does not come from revival. Revival comes from unity. If we want true revival, we must truly want unity at the core of everything we do when we diverge from societal norms and church culture expectations.

In 1906, Charles Parham, a white man, and William Seymour, a black man, both living in the midst of racial segregation in different parts of the United States, simultaneously and prophetically proclaimed that about one hundred years later, a great revival would come. We are in that dispensation of time now—but how do we usher in this massive revival that's coming? I think it lies within the fact that God gave a white man and a black man the same words. We won't see racial reconciliation in our nation until we see it in the Church body. God is not looking for perfection, He's looking for permission. America has an extremely messed up past with slavery, bondage, and prejudicial mindsets. We must choose to remember the past but, God forbid, not relive it! And we must *forgive* it in order for that to happen—not continue propagating it through accepting demonic doctrines steeped in Critical Race Theory.

The emergent divergent is not comprised of white evangelical voices or black evangelical voices. We are not voices for anything but the Kingdom of God. The heart we speak from cannot be about reparation, nor can it be about supremacy. It has to be about unity so that a true revival can take place. Reparation is not reconciliation; it is another form of division. That is, at heart, a spirit of revenge.

The heart of the emergent divergent is to bring all societal factions together to honor the King of kings and the Lord of lords. We are no closer to the nature of Satan than when we accuse the brethren. Unity does not exist in uniformity, but in harmony. It's the black and white notes together that play on the piano to make incredible music. We are all baptized in one Spirit regardless of race. Anything that brings division to the body is straight from the gates of Hell.

About Politics

My wife and I were personally invited to pray at the White House during Donald Trump's presidency. It's an honor to pray with any president who calls with an invitation and asks for prayer. I would pray with that president regardless of whether he or she were Democrat, Republican, Independent, or disagreed with my biblical beliefs. Why? Because God called prophets and renowned men and women of God to speak and pray for leaders of nations throughout the Bible.

Could it be that we're not yet seeing the massive move of God that is ready to be poured out because we're not in the upper room, nor in the prayer room, nor on the threshing floor? Many of us instead are in the political room. Our challenge today is that people are hungrier for the word of Washington, D.C., than they are for the Word of the Lord. Daily, many of us get up and imbibe the word of CNN, Fox News, and other media outlets. *Give us this day our social media. Give us this day our daily news.* It seems many have divided the Church just like they have divided the nation. If you're Republican, you're voting for white people, and if you're Democrat, you're voting for black people. Many even choose their church by its political persuasions or predominant color.

I am not willing to disobey God when it comes to this. I am not a politician. I am not a businessman. I am a preacher, a pastor, and a man of God at the core of my being, and that is what we all should strive to be at the core of whatever title we hold. I do not get to have an opinion as a Christian. Even if persecution comes, I must go with the Word of the Lord. I am unbiased when it comes to praying for people. All people! When God opens the door to pray for someone, our first thoughts cannot be, "Do they go to my type of church?" "What color are they?" "Did they vote the way I did?" Martin Luther King Jr., Billy Graham, and other renowned divergents prayed with people of both parties while in office. Billy

Graham met with every president who served after World War II until his own death. The reason he took a picture with every sitting president was to commemorate a moment, not to complete an agreement!

The emergent divergent are Christians first, and we relinquish ourselves from anything that stokes division in the Body of Christ. If you are political first and a believer second, it's going to be hard to agree with the Word of God that calls on us to pray "for all men; for kings, and for all who are in authority." (1 Timothy 2:1–2 KJV)

The emergent divergent are sent by God to recalibrate the Church. It would appear we have missed the mark of unity widely in the American church. Disunity has caused disability and displacement. *Agape* love goes beyond all color boundaries and is fueled by the Holy Spirit. How can we walk together unless we agree? This is a biblical truth: If there is no agreement, there will be no power!

> "Again I say to you that if two of you agree on earth concerning anything that they ask, it will be done for them by My Father in heaven. For where two or three are gathered together in My name, I am there in the midst of them." (Matthew 18:19–20)

The emergent divergent are called out of a religious system in order to agree to a change. The word "agree" in the Greek is *symphonos*, and it is where we get the word "symphony." If you have ever heard an orchestra while the musicians are rehearsing and tuning up right before a performance, it sounds chaotic. Every section is rehearsing different parts of the music. The trumpets may be on section two while the clarinets are on section five. No one is together. Each person is doing his own thing! However, when the conductor steps out, every section of the orchestra stops and goes to page one of the sheet music. The musicians sit up and get in position, waiting for the conductor to begin. No matter what position you play—first chair, second chair, or third chair of any instrument—everyone has a part. I believe the Conductor of our lives is stepping to the rostrum and calling the emergent divergent voices of our generation to collectively combine and snap into position.

In order to raise the standard, it is mandatory that we raise our voice! We must separate and stand for righteousness with unity so that the rest of the Church can rise up into unity as well. I am praying for this movement to cross all color lines so that we can emerge together: black, white, brown, red, yellow—a glorious Church that is unified beyond any party. A group of *divergents* helps us see that *all* of us are stronger than *any* of us!

CHAPTER 7

THE "REAL" GOD PARTICLE

Invade the Invisible First!

W hen God formed Adam, He took dirt from the ground and shaped it. It lay there, lifeless, until He breathed into the form and made it a living person. Without the breath of God in us, we are nothing but dirt. Period!

> And the LORD GOD formed man out of the dust of the ground, and breathed into his nostrils the breath of life; and man became a living being. (Genesis 2:7)

You Are the Product of a Voice

The European Organization for Nuclear Research (CERN) is an intergovernmental organization that runs a facility in Switzerland that houses the Large Hadron Collider—a machine in which atoms are smashed to discover what actually holds matter together. We know atoms are made of protons, neutrons, and electrons; what is inside them?

In its quest to find out how the earth formed and the universe began, CERN has sent protons in opposite directions, accelerated the particles, and then smashed them together to create a tiny version of the Big Bang to find out what holds the earth and us together. The results were staggering: The researchers found something they called a "quark," which is essentially an electric vibration. In other words, something invisible created the visible. So what holds this world together? Something that has vibration.

"Sound" is created when air passes through an instrument or a vocal fold. Sound is air with vibration. When we talk to one another, we are listening to air passing through vibration, shaped into words by a mouth. Try it. First, breathe with no sound. Then open your mouth and breathe, only making vibrations through your vocal cords. Now begin to move your mouth and tongue to shape the words. Scientists spent multiple millions of dollars to verify that Someone spoke matter into existence.

> God, having spoken to the fathers long ago in [the voices and writings of] the prophets in many separate revelations [each of which set forth a portion of the truth], and in many ways, has in these last days spoken [with finality] to us in [the person of One who is by His character and nature] His Son [namely Jesus], whom He appointed heir and lawful owner of all things, *through whom also He created the universe [that is, the universe as a space-time-matter continuum]*. The Son is the radiance and only

expression of the glory of [our awesome] God [reflecting God's Shekinah glory, the Light-being, the brilliant light of the divine], and the exact representation and perfect imprint of His [Father's] essence, and *upholding and maintaining and propelling all things* [*the entire physical and spiritual universe*] *by His powerful word* [*carrying the universe along to its predetermined goal*]. (Hebrews 1:1–3; AMP, emphasis added)

For since the creation of the world His *invisible attributes are clearly seen,* being understood by the things that are made, even His eternal power and Godhead, so that they are without excuse. (Romans 1:20; emphasis added)

Everything that we "clearly see" comes from something that we cannot see! This means we are products of an invisible world. Hebrews 11:1–3 discusses in depth what *faith* really is and how this invisible world relates to us:

Now faith is the substance of things hoped for, the evidence of things not seen. For by it the elders obtained a good testimony. By faith we understand that the worlds were framed by the word of God, so that the things which are seen were not made of things which are visible.

Why does this matter? (No pun intended.) Everything you see is a product of vibration. Someone spoke all of this into existence. The Bible refers to the Godhead as the beginning of everything.

The Spirit of God hovered over the face of the deep, and then God spoke. John 1 tells us that in the beginning was the "Word," and the Word was with God and the Word was God. That means Jesus, God, and the Holy Spirit lived in perfect unity before the first words were ever spoken into this earth. God said, "Let there be light," and there was light! God spoke it into existence, and then He saw what He spoke. God did not have to *possess* faith, God *is* faith.

The same thing happened with Mary's pregnancy when she was to carry Jesus, the Son of God. The Spirit of God hovered over her and then impregnated her with the *Word!*

Genesis tells us that we are created in His image and have the ability to create with our words as well. Hebrews 11:1 tells us that our faith is substance. The substance of what? Things hoped for! *What we believe will happen; it is the evidence of things not seen!*

Your Voice Belongs to the Invisible World

I can see my physical self, the body that God spoke into existence. A doctor can open me up and see every part of me that was formed and is now visible. There's only one part of me that no one can see, because that part belongs to an invisible world: You cannot see my voice. You can only hear it and feel its effects.

So, just like God, our dominion comes from our voice. Your words belong to the invisible world, the supernatural. You cannot fight the invisible world with visible things. This is why Jesus Himself fought the devil with the Word of God. There was no hand-to-hand combat, wrestling match, or a UFC challenge. No, He fought him with invisible words.

If invisible words created everything you see, wouldn't it be important to note that the product of our voices might be that powerful as well? We wrestle not against flesh and blood, but against powers, principalities, and rulers.

> For we do not wrestle against flesh and blood, but against principalities, against powers, against the rulers of the darkness of this age, against spiritual hosts of wickedness in heavenly places. (Ephesians 6:12)

What does this mean? We don't fight physically. We fight spiritually. Satan does not have the power of God. God has no equal. Satan is *our* enemy. The Bible says woe unto the inhabitants of the earth, for Satan has come down to you! It also calls Satan the prince of the power of the *air!*

> In which you once walked according to the course of this world, according to the prince of the power of the air, the spirit who now works in the sons of disobedience. (Ephesians 2:2)

Your Voice Has Power

While Satan is a prince, God has given you *kingly* rule and has made us (note the past tense) kings and priests, according to the Word. Through the name of Jesus, we are seated in the heavenly realms of His authority. Satan has no power or authority for someone who walks in the power of the name of Jesus Christ. Our words are powerful. Our words are not meant simply to amaze people; they are laden with authority.

When Jesus was twelve years old, priests heard Him speaking and were astonished by His words because they possessed authority! Authority represents delegated power to act. It's the same word used in Luke 9 when Jesus tells His disciples to drive out demons and lay hands on the sick. God has given us authority through our voice. James speaks of our tongue being like a rudder on a ship that turns it where it needs to go.

Chuck Yeager, the first person to break the sound barrier, struggled for a long time before he did it. Think about that. Every time he tried, his plane shook violently, nearly to the point of disassembling itself. Many scientists and engineers thought the sound barrier could not be broken with current technology. Frustrated by this, Yeager went back to the plane's designer, Jack Ridley, and asked him to make one small modification to the back of the plane: the rudder. With that one small adjustment, the shaking lessened, and he broke the sound barrier.

Our words and tongues are powerful, just like the rudder on that plane. One small adjustment, and we can change the whole world. This is why I am *begging* the remnant to raise its voice! Our words are invisible, but they shape the places we live. Our words are so powerful that we are held accountable even to the empty words we speak.

> "But I say to you that for every idle word men may speak, they will give account of in the day of judgment."
> (Matthew 12:36)

Your Voice Brings Life

Jesus says our words bring life.

> "It is the Spirit who gives life; the flesh profits nothing. The words that I speak to you are spirit, and they are life." (John 6:63)

Jesus says the *words* (the invisible) that He speaks are *zoe*—physical life. Think about the woman with the issue of blood. For twelve years—144 months—she sat with this issue! How did she get her miracle? What changed? The Bible says, "She said within herself…" She spoke out and *told herself*, "I will be healed if I touch even the hem of His garment." And she was healed!

The centurion said the same thing to Jesus: "I know that if you will speak a word, my servant will be healed because I am a man in authority." Jesus's response was, "This is great *faith*." Understand the Word, and you will understand how the invisible changes the visible. You are not a physical being having a spiritual experience; you are a spiritual being having a physical experience. When we speak, it changes things. We must speak now, or we won't be allowed to later!

Everything we see is the product of a voice—first God's, then yours! When God finished creating via speaking, He rested. That's what He is doing right now. Everything you see that has been created is what will be used to create more things. God passed the baton of creation into the words of human beings. If you want to see something happen, you've got to speak it out—first to yourself, and then to others.

There is no authority on this earth unless you are a speaking, breathing being. Think about it. What's the first thing that goes away when you die? Your breath. As long as you're breathing, you have authority in this visible world.

God always speaks through a voice in authority to bring order in this world. Satan is not a planter. He is a supplanter! He jumps on property that doesn't rightfully belong to him and illegally operates from it. He is not an originator; he just perverts the original purpose of God. He makes us believe that what God said is not what He really meant!

Listen to how Satan twisted it all! In Genesis 2, something changes concerning how we identify God. The book begins by identifying Him as "the Lord God," yet when Satan speaks to Eve, he only calls him "God."

The word *Yahweh* means "Lord." The word *Elohim* means "God."

If You Are Breathing, You Have Dominion

Why is that important? Even Satan acknowledges that there is a God, but the word "Lord" represents authority.

It has been said that the word *Yahweh*—in the original text, without the vowels—sounds like breathing. Take a moment to breathe in and then out without using words. When you breathe in, you will hear the word "Yah" and when you breathe out, you will hear the word "way." Even the most atheistic of atheists declares the Lord every time he breathes. (Side note: This is why Psalm 150 says to let everything that has *breath* praise the Lord.) *Every breath we take is designed to irritate the devil.* All he can hear is, "Yahweh,

Yahweh, Yahweh"! As long as you are breathing, you remind the enemy that God is Lord!

Oh, how the enemy wants us to be disobedient to God's authority! He hates that your voice, even while breathing, denotes that, "God is Lord." He's after your voice. It is impossible for you to talk without breath. Your words need the breath of God in them.

Look at what Eve did when she saw that the tree was "good" to eat. Why did she pay attention to what God said not to touch? Because she heard a voice; the serpent began to speak to her. *Who is speaking to you?* It's very important that you understand that whoever has your ear has your future. *Good* is not always good. We begin to operate in disobedience when we listen to voices that disagree with God.

Both Eve and Adam turned away from God's accountability and felt their way was better, so they ate the forbidden fruit. After that, they saw themselves differently. They became ashamed and sewed fig leaves together to cover their private parts. Why do they cover their nakedness? I truly believe one of the greatest things the enemy does not like about us is the fact that we can be procreative, that we can populate and colonize the Kingdom of God on this earth. Satan cannot create. He can only pervert creation.

The word of God in your voice is just as powerful as the word of God in Jesus's voice.

Jesus told us the works that He did are great, but we would do greater works. Then He went on to explain, "Because I go to the Father in Heaven." Jesus is currently sitting at the right hand of the Father in His sovereign rule in Heaven. However, His Body is functioning on this earth. We are the Body of Christ. We do greater works not because we're greater than Jesus, but because we are an extension of Him upon the earth. We are not in Heaven yet, and many things have yet to happen. Why doesn't Jesus Himself just come down to do them? He will; that's called the Second Coming. But until then, He has given mankind authority to operate through the Holy Spirit.

What I am about to say does not mean that God is not sovereign, but it needs to be clarified: No spirit has access to move in authority unless a body is present. If God's Word, His voice, is all powerful—which it is—then Satan understands that as well. God cannot lie. Everything God says comes into being. He watches over His words because He is bound by His Word. Why is this important? He made one pronouncement about the whole human race. Satan heard this in Genesis.

> Then God said, "Let Us make man in Our image, according to Our likeness; let them have dominion over the fish of the sea, over the birds of the air, and over the cattle, over all the earth and over every creeping thing that creeps on the earth." (Genesis 1:26)

Let them have dominion. Where? On the earth. In order to have dominion on this earth, you have to be a human. Dead people have no authority. The moment you stop breathing, you lose authority to change anything on this earth. We must believe in the voice that God has given us in order to bring change to our culture.

The disciples asked Jesus in Matthew 17, "Why could we not cast the demon out?" He said, "Because of the mountain of unbelief." Then He began to teach them how to walk in faith.

"For assuredly, I say to you, if you have faith as a mustard seed, you will say to this mountain, 'Move from here to there,' and it will move; and nothing will be impossible for you." (Matthew 17:20)

Jesus said something similar concerning the fig tree that withered:

"Have faith in God. For assuredly, *I say to you, whoever says to this* mountain, 'Be removed and be cast into the sea,' and does not doubt in his heart, but believes that those things he says will be done, he will have whatever he says. Therefore I say to you, whatever things you ask when you pray, believe that you receive them, and you will have them." (Mark 11:22–24; emphasis added)

Our faith, our voice, is like that mustard seed. It's really not about the size, it's the conviction in it. The mustard seed never changes what it knows it is, even when it is buried deep in the ground. It doesn't change its convictions when it emerges and the storms meet it. The mustard seed continues to believe that it is what God created it to be. Jesus said, "This is the faith you must have in your heart concerning the words of God." Let your voice agree with God's words.

The lesson of the fig tree is just as powerful concerning our voice. Jesus starts by saying, "Have faith in God." If our faith is attached to our words, this scripture should validate it. He said, "I say to you, 'Say to this…'" It's words! Let the weak *say*, "I am strong." Let the poor *say*, "I am rich." "Whoever *says* to the mountain…"

So why am I writing about that? Because if we're going to see any change in our world, it's going to come from a spiritual place. *Faith comes to us by hearing, but faith goes from us by speaking.* If we're going to change the world we live in, we must begin to speak out.

Censorship is the beginning of perse-CUT-ion. *Cut!* Before a society cancels your influence as a Christian, it will cancel your voice. It will attempt to cancel your ability to speak what you believe. This is what is happening right now on social media. You are penalized if you write or say anything the masses classify as hate. What I have learned is that most of what is being called "hate speech" comes straight from the Word of God. How can soft porn, sexual perversion, satanic symbolism, and racist speech be acceptable on the social media platforms, but some scriptures will immediately be shadow-banned or deleted? Not only that, but the overseers will warn you that if you make another offensive post, *you* will be deleted. If they can take away your voice, they can take away your influence. The Word of God is offensive to those who don't like truth.

So, what do we do? Fight! Fight for your freedom of speech. This is so fundamental to freedom that our forefathers of America put it in the First Amendment to the Constitution. Ours is a *free* country. *We are free to speak.*

The Second Amendment guarantees the right to take up something with which to defend yourself. Our forefathers shook off tyranny in the Declaration of *Independence*. Those voices that spoke more than two hundred years ago are still being challenged. You must enforce the freedoms God has given you. Our voice as a remnant must rise up and speak the heart of God, the *true freedom* that belongs to humanity, in the name of Jesus.

The enemy wants your voice silenced in the nations—but first he wants to silence it in your head! He wants you to doubt and be irritated by your own voice. Also, be careful of those who are intoxicated by the sound of their own voice. People like this are typically notorious narcissists. The Kingdom is about them, not about God. They speak to impress themselves.

Your voice holds things in place. I think about Joshua, a man who spoke up and told the sun to stand still. I think about Elijah, who told the rain to hold off for three and a half years. God did not ask them to speak, but their words commanded those things to happen, and God agreed with them. *Most of us don't struggle to believe that God's voice is for us, but rather with the idea that God's voice will speak through us.* If we are going to see our society return to morality, it will come by the voice of God speaking through us, changing the regime.

God backs your voice when you speak in faith and agree with His Word. There is a high anointing on your voice when you cry out in such a way. The enemy is not bothered by what you believe or which church you belong to. He is bothered by your accepting the truth and then speaking it with your mouth. You have authority; Satan doesn't when we decree and dictate the voice of God on the earth.

Even our salvation is a product of our confession. Your voice is so powerful that if you confess with your mouth and believe in your heart that Jesus is Lord, you shall be saved. We have a voice, and it needs to be heard.

We must stop allowing ourselves to be defined by what the world says and start defining the world by what God says. *Your voice makes the difference between confusion and clarity.* Make a clarion call right now with your voice. Lift it up like a trumpet. Rally the troops with a sound! Let the trumpet of your mouth make a certain sound that rallies the troops to move forward. I refuse for the Body of Christ to retreat from this war raging within society and culture. Our children deserve better. Raise your voice and speak now, or forever hold your peace.

CHAPTER 8

RALLY THE REMNANT

A Bold and Fearless Militia Is Forming

Since the Bible mentions "the remnant" 540 times, it's important for us to know exactly what a remnant is.

The remnant of God is an army of believers "inside" the Church, not exempt or excluded from it. They are not better than anyone; they are just bolder than most. They are normal, everyday people, but they are vocal about God's heart—a Special Ops unit within the Church that is deadly to the kingdom of darkness. They are soldiers. They are completely committed to the Word of God and will be a voice for Him, come hell or high water. They don't relent. They are not moved by praise or criticism. They not only speak of God, but for God, and they refuse to bow to anything that culture or religion wants them to unethically tolerate. They will not retreat—even if it means misunderstanding, punishment, imprisonment, persecution, and, yes, even death.

What are the remnant *not?* They are not rebels, renegades, or radicals. They are normal people who are offended by what offends God.

We need an army in God's Church right now that will procure a revival of sanity and sanctification, not only in the streets but also in the sanctuary. A remnant that is not afraid to raise its voice for the sake of getting the Church back to the governance of God through Jesus Christ. It is of utmost importance to our generation and the coming generation that we speak up.

Call Up the Reserve. We Are in a War!

The word for remnant is "reserve." In Paul's discourse to the Romans, he gives us this quote from the Old Testament concerning Elijah's conversation with God on Mount Horeb after Elijah called fire down from Heaven and ended a three-and-a-half-year drought. Elijah's next move was not to give a victory speech or launch a social media marketing campaign about what God did. No, it was to flee to a cave to escape Jezebel's murder decree. (Side note: The spirit of Jezebel is as active today as it was thousands of years ago. She is named "cancel culture" to the prophets' voice, and manifests most often as sexual perversion. She has a way of making the majority go with her.)

Paul told the Romans,

> God has not cast away His people whom He foreknew.
> Or do you not know what the Scripture says of Elijah,
> how he pleads with God against Israel, saying, "LORD,
> they have killed Your prophets and torn down Your

altars, and I alone am left, and they seek my life"? But what does the divine response say to him? "I have *reserved for Myself seven thousand men* who have not bowed the knee to Baal." Even so then, at this present time there is a remnant according to the election of grace. (Romans 11:2–5; emphasis added)

A reserve! An army! That is militant! In America we have Army Reserve soldiers. They receive the same training as active-duty soldiers, such as basic combat training and advanced individual training, but they are also civilians. After boot camp, they spend one weekend a month and two weeks a year training to keep their skills sharp. A reservist knows he could be called upon at any time to safeguard the nation, but until that time, he may attend college, pursue a career, and raise a family. However, reservists know that when danger hits the shores of their country and overwhelms the active armed forces, they are fully trained and ready to go. Right now in America, there are close to two hundred thousand reserves who at any moment, if called on, are ready to go to battle.

God has a reserve. He has a remnant. They're not just preachers behind the pulpit. They are ordinary people who are ready to be actively deployed in spiritual warfare to protect and defend the Church of God. They are working in the marketplace, attending college, and raising families, but they're also deeply engaged in the matters of spiritual warfare.

I have noticed in my travels that there are many people fed up with immorality in church as well as in the nations. I've seen ex-gang members, tradesmen and -women, mothers, fathers, and businesspeople who don't look like typical churchgoers begin to raise their voices as the remnant of God. You will recognize the remnant by their voice, not their outfit or church affiliation. As a matter of fact, they are affiliated with many churches that may seem to be dying. They speak up and are loud when God calls upon them!

A remnant is a reserve with a voice nobody wants to hear until everybody needs to hear it. When I was growing up, I had a three-wheeler. As a teenager, I would fill up the gas tank and go hit the trails behind my house. I had so much fun that sometimes I would go farther than I should have, and many times I ran out of gas because I wasn't paying attention. I would be rolling along, jumping dirt piles, and suddenly, my three-wheeler would come to a stop. You get a little nervous when you are a young boy way out from home with no gas. Then I would remember what my father told me to do if that happened. He said to reach down below the tank to a silver switch that can point to three conditions:

1. Gas on
2. Gas off
3. Reserve

My father told me that if I ever get too far from home and ran out of gas to switch to the *reserve* and come *straight home.* This was fuel to be used in emergencies. Don't veer off the road, don't go out to play again, don't go anywhere else—come straight home! The gas in the reserve was the same gas found in the rest of the tank, just saved for emergencies!

Well, we have an emergency! The nation's decline of morality, the sexual deviancy with which our children are being indoctrinated at school, and the churches turning away from God's moral principles across the nation require a *reserve.*

The remnant's responsibility is to get people back home.

When the Church gets too far out, seeking the world's approval rather than separating from it, God calls in the remnant. They are loud and don't care about offending people. Their goal is to get the Church back to the heart of God. When we mix our convictions with compromise and say God condones sinful behavior, He calls out the remnant forces to speak up and not relent. The remnant doesn't care if you cancel them. They are going to speak anyway. They are bent on turning people from their wicked ways.

Let me share with you the good, the bad, and the ugly of remnant life.

UGLY: There has never been a darker time in our history. The mocking of Jesus is at an all-time high. Why are celebrities and other public figures not mocking Muhammad, Buddha, other gods? Because none of those other gods are a threat to Satan—only Jesus is. You have Taylor Swift telling people to calm down and mocking Christians for standing against the LGBTQ agenda.[1] You have Lil Nas X twerking on the lap of Satan, mocking Jesus, and then releasing a shoe line with pentagram pendants, human blood in the soles, and a reference to Luke 10:18 (referencing Lucifer's fall from Heaven).[2] You have Sam Smith and Kim Petras—an openly gay man and a transgender "woman"—pantomiming an entire satanic ritual on stage at the Grammy Awards while singing a song called "Unholy."[3] You have Beyonce singing that she uses pages from the Bible as tampons.[4] You have Nickelodeon and *Blue's Clues* leading more than two million children to sing along with a song praising LGBTQ inclusion.[5] You have the marketing of "Holy Spirit Ouija Boards."[6]

When Jesus is openly mocked at the level we have seen over the last few years—and Satan openly worshiped—it shows us what the heart of a nation looks like. After all, no one is censoring it, and many of the examples I just mentioned have millions of views. Some of those views are from regular churchgoers who don't seem to be bothered by it—or if they are, they are saying nothing! That's the ugly.

THE BAD: The remnant is smaller than anyone thinks. The church in America has declined by 76 percent in only two years. With 338 million people in America and only 24 percent actually in the army (Church) of God, how many are a remnant? Who knows? Remember that a remnant is a small portion of the whole.

THE GOOD: Fortunately, the size of a remnant means nothing—it's about the conviction. While the remnant is smaller than you think, it is stronger than you think! Being holy enough is not the catalyst for the type of culture shift we need; being hungry enough is! The remnant now is hungry. The Spirit is pouring out on the hungry. Those who hunger and thirst *after righteousness* shall be filled. This move of the Holy Spirit we are in is going to those who are willing to be hungry. Many are gathering now on college campuses, churches, and other places that hunger for righteousness.

Whether it's Elijah or seven thousand fellow prophets, God is looking for somebody who will speak for Him. Show me where God went over to the side of the majority in the Bible. Show me where it ever worked for the Church to partner with the world in order to win the lost. Jesus sat with sinners but never sinned with them. God had Gideon whittle his army down to three hundred men and gave him a great victory. God sent one man named Moses to deliver millions out of bondage and slavery.

While many people will look to the majority to see what is popular and assume that God is somehow in it, the remnant looks to the Word of the Lord to see what God is saying *in spite of* popular trends. The fact that popular people say something that sounds religious doesn't mean it comes from God.

God, deliver us from some of these celebrity Christian leaders who have no heart for You! More than that, God, deliver us from the foolishness of listening to those who are bent on compromising morality for the sake of church growth. *God is not pleased with us when our only aspirations for Christianity are for it to be popular, accepted by the world, and comfortable.*

I had a plaque on my desk for many years that read, "No one is stronger than the weakest person who is totally dependent upon God." That rings true for the remnant. We are totally dependent upon Him and His Word. We have no desire to stand back, shut up, or be silent because we are totally sold out to God. We can't hold our tongues when we see the onslaught of *unrighteous* activity in the house of God and in our nation. *God moves in authority, not majority.* Again, God is not looking for the majority's vote. His Kingdom is not a democracy. His Kingdom is one of sovereign authority. When God cannot find somebody in His own Church to raise his voice against immorality, injustice, and perversion, He will raise up somebody else, put a burden on him, and release him to speak on His behalf. *God always has a person or people who will speak for Him.*

We are walking dead men. We have died to the desire for popularity and worrying about what others think. We have died to the desire to be praised by man. If it smells like compromise, we won't even go near it.

A. W. Tozer said, "We cannot afford to let down our Christian standards just to hold the interest of people who want to go to hell and still belong to a church."[7]

I'm telling you, the remnant are bold! If you are part of it, it comes with the great price of being misunderstood. The table that you never sit at is the comfort-TABLE. You will be misunderstood by the Church first and the world second. But the Church will eventually understand why you speak so violently for God's ways of righteousness. They will call holiness legalism. They will call being separate from the world being divisive. This attitude is driven by greed and compromise, maybe even secret sin that doesn't want to be found out. I have heard through the years that the people who preach grace only are typically the people who need it the most. I'm not against grace preaching, I'm against grace-without-truth preaching.

The remnant is a small yet deadly force on the earth doing the Lord's work. *For God has reserved you! All of heaven is standing, not waiting on the return of the Lord, but the return of the Church.* It's going to take a remnant to step out in authority and speak to things that are not as they ought to be. The remnant will not be the most celebrated by man, but Heaven will back their words. Even though there has never been a darker time, there has also never been a greater time for an outpouring of the Holy Ghost.

In the same story of Elijah mentioned above, he speaks of a rain coming and hears it in his spirit days before it happens. But he *did not see* the outpouring until he dealt with the evils of his day. It wasn't until after he called fire down from Heaven and killed the prophets of Baal that the outpouring began. The same will happen with the outpouring of our day.

Elijah went to the top of Mount Carmel, bowed down, and put his face between his knees to pray. *Why? Because nothing starts pouring until someone starts praying.* God's house is a house of prayer. That is what Jesus said. While other parts of a service are important, like giving, singing, preaching, etc., Jesus didn't say that God's house is a house of preaching, singing, entertaining, or anything else. The rain fell because there was a praying man. I truly believe that *what has been put on pause is about to pour because of the prayers of the righteous!*

Change is coming! Elijah sent his servant to look for a cloud—not once, but seven times before that servant came back and said, "There is a cloud the size of a man's hand." I believe the clouds were begging for the voice of Elijah. Elijah was not waiting on the clouds; the clouds were waiting on Elijah. In the same manner, we are not waiting on revival, revival is waiting on us. We are the revival—the *ruach*, the very breath of God on this earth.

A voice for the remnant of God will have these convictions:

1. A remnant cannot be bought and is turned off by the very mention of it.
2. A remnant will stick with the Word and separate from the world.
3. A remnant will live with heavy conviction and will demonstrate God's Word.
4. A remnant is not a voice for the evangelical right or for the liberal left. It is a voice for the Lord of Hosts (Isaiah 1:9).
5. A remnant not only preaches truth, but truth and love.

The Church will misunderstand you at first. *I repeat: You will be misunderstood!* Many people misunderstand the remnant as judgmental. Remember David showing up when Goliath was taunting the Israelite army? His own family misunderstood him and told him to go home. But David said, *"Is there not a cause?"* He showed up with stones to the battle. Even King Saul tried to discredit him. The king said, "Fight with my armor, a shield, a sword; after all this is what we always use to fight with!" But David said, "No, I've not proven these." Reluctantly, the king agreed to send a small shepherd boy out against the mighty Goliath with no armor on—nothing that resembled the rest of the army . . . or the Church.

People are going to misunderstand your stones. There's a difference between throwing stones and slinging them, and some will not understand what it is until you roll the head off the giant. Yet there's a cause that is greater than the misunderstanding of even those you labor with. Love all people, yes, but refuse to be silent when Goliath shows up. Throwing stones typically means people feel judged, but slinging stones means taking down giants. The remnant are slinging stones! That means we're dealing with something that's stopping the people of God from moving forward. There is so much in the Church that is hindering the true move of God. Mixture with the world—or conversely, a desire to live so apart from the world that we don't affect it at all—and an apathetic approach to pursuing godliness and holiness are some of them. Stones have to be slung at the enemy to announce to him that we will fight back.

Sometimes when correcting a child, coddling is not appropriate. When we want serious change out of our child, it requires a stronger approach. *God can't coddle and correct an apathetic Church with no appetite for doing right.* He spits our lukewarm agendas out.

All of this talk about awakening and revival won't happen until we cry out for God to send a voice—and that voice typically doesn't sound like something the church culture wants to hear. Don't misunderstand the voices or the stones. *We must become insulted by the things that insult God, even at the cost of church or family discomfort.* The remnant of God is not called to comfort people. The reserve is called up because the army is overwhelmed and in trouble. We are a militia; common people with a set-in-stone conviction to defend what God has entrusted to us. We will beat our plows into spears and fight for the cause of Christ's awesome Church on Earth!

We are the remnant. We cannot keep quiet. We refuse to give one inch to the devil, even if it goes against the majority. For twenty years, we have used our faith as a service to ourselves rather than as a shield for the Body to quench the enemy's fiery darts. The shield of faith is not meant to simply bless us; it exists to *block attacks* from the evil one.

I don't believe in the prosperity gospel; I believe in a gospel that has prosperity in it. When we only use our faith to call things in, we are left with a selfish gospel—and that is the exact opposite of the Gospel of Jesus Christ. That is religion at its finest. Religion is nothing but dry bones and dirty dishes without revival. The remnant refuses to allow dry bones to be the definition of God's anointed Church. We aren't interested in the appearance of godliness without the power! No! We refuse to allow powerless, lifeless existences to be the sign of a believer in Christ!

When a fiery dart lodges in the body, it begins to create infection and a loss of power. How do you know people are lifeless? They won't respond to *anything*. They're numb! Unresponsiveness is a sign that there is a need to be revived. How quiet the mainstream church has become in this season concerning sin and compromise! When the Church becomes unresponsive to sin, the EKG monitor cannot be trusted. At this point, we need someone to manually check the pulse.

I believe God has His hand on the neck of the Church, looking for a pulse today. If He cannot find a pulse, He will reach for the defibrillator. If the remnant were a piece of medical equipment, it would be the defibrillator. When CPR doesn't work, massaging the heart doesn't work, and the pulse monitor still says there isn't one, then bring out the defibrillator.

There are moments in the Church's life when breathing and pumping a regular routine of church programs won't get the job done. You're gonna have to shock the Body. You're going to need jumper cables that are attached to a different source—a battery pack that is fully charged. That is a remnant. They may seem the same as others, but when God has need of them, they will shock the Body. The Body of Christ needs shock therapy. If we don't get it, there will be brain damage—that is, the Body won't be able to think clearly. The world will begin forming its thoughts rather than the Word.

But the remnant will not allow that to happen. Like a paramedic baring the chest, we will strip away whatever is blocking our ability to shock you. We're not doing it because we are mad; we are doing it because we want life to return to the Body. The remnant refuses to play church or go along with anything that keeps us in the grave clothes of religion. You will live again! You will be an army! You will get your voice back, and your children will be blessed by it!

It's time! It's actually past time for the voice of God to resonate on this earth. It's more than just a need for revival—we need revolt! We need a resurgent, revolutionary remnant that grasps the desperate need for the revival of a forcible Church that takes back spiritual property and extinguishes wicked agendas and man-made programs with a mantle from God. Revival is not pretty, but it is powerful. Paramedics don't show up in order to show off their outfits or the latest and greatest equipment. No, they are there to bring the body back to life!

Christians are the most persecuted people in the world. Let that sink in. In America, nothing is truly felt until it troubles us immediately and personally. Many people have a cause or concern, but when you are a remnant, you have a *burden*. This is different. Some people in the Church don't even realize that they *are* the remnant until what is happening in the world begins to affect them personally. It's as if this wakes them up from the weakness of woke-ness. Then they have a burden, because their eyes are opened. No longer do they go to church to hear the Word of the Lord quoted by someone else, they get in the Word for themselves and soon realize that His Word does not evolve, even if the world seems to. That's why the Word of God is called a "standard"! It doesn't change. It's the plumb line.

God has a voice in our nation, and it needs to be heard. After living under years of immoral indoctrination through all types of media and education, it's our turn. When 5 percent of the people in a group begin to say the same thing, leaders will wake up and listen. There is a window for the remnant's voice to be heard. We must refuse to allow any ungodly education, unholy politics, or the unrighteous mountains of media and the arts to raise our children! We must fight back, and we must fight right. The remnant does not fight in the natural; it fights in the spiritual. That does not mean we sit quietly in a corner and pray only. It means we fight against powers and principalities by lifting our voice and claiming our children back with the righteousness of God.

It's time to rally the remnant. Nothing will change until we rally. Wickedness, lawlessness, and unrighteousness will prevail with apparently overwhelming strength until we rally. But if we rally, that devil is going to listen to us and do what we say!

> "Wherever you hear the sound of the trumpet, rally to us there. Our God will fight for us." (Nehemiah 4:20)

Nehemiah knew all too well he had to stop building the walls when the enemy came in. Wherever you are stationed, lay down your tools and rally with the Church. Even if the cost is substantial—rally. The remnant *must rally*. The world has unleashed Hell because our enemy, Satan, knows his time is short. We must unleash Heaven's Kingdom on the earth. God has given us keys and told us that "whatever you bind on earth will be bound in heaven, and whatever you loose on earth will be loosed in heaven" (Matthew 16:19). These are the rightful keys of authority that God gave us at the beginning. These are part of His definition of what the Church is. The gates of Hell cannot prevail against us.

Remnant, raise your voice and rally the Church together. Let's change the nations for the glory of God and for the sake of our children!

CHAPTER 9

GAP MEN

Stand between Heaven and Earth, and Speak Up

When I look at the word "gap," I see an acronym: God's Anointed Preachers.

This chapter is going to pour fuel on your prayer life. It's going to stir you up to raise your voice. Jesus Himself refused to minister without the baptism of the Holy Spirit. The moment God's Spirit rested on Him in the form of a dove after His water baptism, He stood in the gap between Heaven and Earth as the greatest intercessory preacher who ever lived.

We are called to be "gap men," too. Oh, to be baptized in the Holy Spirit! When you get saved, Heaven knows your name, but when you get baptized in the Holy Ghost, Hell knows your name.

Social media gives us a glimpse of what people truly want you to celebrate. Sometimes it's subtle, but sometimes it's blatant. I've never seen so many heavy-drinking believers, abortion-supporting congregants, fornicating ministers, pedophile preachers, drag-queen celebrators, or LGTBQ-friendly churches in my lifetime. We have worship leaders who want to collaborate with erotic, demonic, and sexually explicit artists in the name of grace and inclusion, and this has increased exponentially over the last five years. Our churches have become a friendly environment for the devil. I am convinced that the devil himself is starting to enjoy the American Church. I am also convinced that Satan has built a few churches himself—especially where I live in Atlanta! There are church leaders who actually *condone* racism and support gay marriage. These leaders teach a heretical doctrine that celebrates men having sex with men and women having sex with women. We have psychics in the church. Society is calling these "gifts to the Body of Christ." Our city has well-known Pentecostal ministers, respected by many, who are known heretics yet are still influential voices to God's people, calling what is wrong right in God's eyes; they twist the Word and stand in the gap for Satan.

Oh yes, Satan has gap men, too! They are fallen angels, embodied in fallen people, that transform themselves into angels of light in order to accomplish hidden darkness. But like Moses, when the staffs are thrown down at the showdown, *the God-anointed preachers*—the GAP MEN—have staffs that will swallow up the staffs of the enemy.

> And no wonder! For Satan transforms himself into an Angel of light. Therefore it is no great thing if *his ministers also transform themselves* into ministers of righteousness, whose end will be according to their works. (2 Corinthians 11:14–15; emphasis added)

Gap men are not chosen because they are worthy. They are chosen because they are willing. They care nothing about titles, invitations to preach, or peer recognition. They have one thing in mind: *God, spare Your people!*

God is after a voice that will stand in the gap for this generation. A voice that will weep, cry, and call out to God on behalf of the people and raise a voice to the people on behalf of God. *This is not a comfortable place.* The gap is lonely, burdensome, and visually depressing, but at the same time, it's fulfilling because you know that you are in the middle of Heaven, interceding on the earth, while the bowels of Hell are breaking loose.

Intercessors stand in the middle. I cannot express how important it is to stand in the middle when you are a voice for God. Isaiah 64 talks about how God is the Potter, and we are the clay. When God picks you from the shelf, you're nothing but a lump of clay. He then puts you on the middle of the pottery wheel. If the clay doesn't stay in the middle of the wheel as God applies pressure to form and create capacity in you, His vessel, the clay will lose its shape and fail. It will be useless.

First of all, be glad that God chose you while other bars of clay were sitting on the shelf. You're on the wheel. In the middle is where you will feel the pressure. There's no capacity without pressure in the middle. The Potter's Wheel is not glamorous, it's grueling. It's a place where the clay still has no clue what it will become, yet has to remain still in the middle while being formed. You are nothing but dirt that is formed to reveal the glory of God. Stay in the middle. You are clay in God's hands, but on Earth you are a vessel that God is forming to fill.

Let the priests, the ministers of the LORD, weep between the porch and the altar, and let them say, Spare thy people, O LORD, and give not thine heritage to reproach, that the heathen should rule over them: wherefore should they say among the people, Where is their God? (Joel 2:17 KJV)

And I sought for a man among them, that should make up the hedge, and stand in the gap before me for the land, that I should not destroy it: but I found none. (Ezekiel 22:30 KJV)

I found none! Wow. My answer to that scripture is, *Not in this generation!* God is raising up a voice that will stand between the people and the altar and compel them to come. We need true *Voices* who will champion the cause of Christ in this generation. You will weep as you occupy a place where you watch the people of God—not just the world, but God's people (*"spare thy people"*)—incriminate themselves with foolish lusts; a place where folly and false freedoms invade the hearts of compromised believers. "If My people would turn from their wicked ways" (see 2 Chronicles 7:14)!

God is after you! He is after a voice that will stand in the gap.

For the eyes of the LORD run to and fro throughout the whole earth, to show Himself strong on behalf of those whose heart is loyal to Him. (2 Chronicles 16:9)

God is looking for someone who will listen to what He is saying. He is always looking for someone to carry the burden of His will on this earth—someone who will eat locusts and wild honey, build an ark, or stand in front of a pharaoh and say, "Let my people go!" He is looking for someone who will stand for God when others are bowing before men, one who doesn't have to have all the pleasures in the world to do His will. It was said of Moses that he chose to suffer affliction rather than bask in the passing pleasures of this world—and he did this for the sake of standing in the gap.

The Call to Intercede

Intercession is an inward desire, a call, as God leads you to become a powerful voice for Him. You move from crawling to standing. Standing means not bowing to the demands of anyone or any expectation of the majority.

The gap is not a place where many want to stand. Zechariah was stoned in this very place by standing against the religious system of his day. *Webster's Dictionary* defines the word "stand" as being "upright on one's feet, steadfast, firm and secure, as pillars stand on each side of the doorway." Standing will require you to hold weight. The weight you will hold is the glory of God!

The gap is where you can't reach the altar and you can't reach the people. You can only stand in the middle and weep. The anointing of the one who cries takes place here, and it is a deep intercession. Driven by the immorality of man, it occurs especially within God's Church.

The porch was once the place where people congregated. Our children, spouses, friends, family, neighbors, coworkers, church members, and the community waited here! It was a common space. It still is. Most people stand here, not in the gap. The altar was a place of sacrifice—a place where you would lose something. It was not a comfortable place, but a place of repentance and reconciliation. The gap was the place where intercessors stood. Again, you can't touch God, and you can't touch the people there; *all you have is a voice!*

Every generation has a gap, and every generation has a voice. The gap the Bible describes is an area in the Temple thirty-three feet wide: 16.5 feet from the porch, 16.5 feet from the altar. In that place, you have to preach to get results. The separation is too far to reach out and grab somebody, yet near enough for others to hear you speak.

Preaching intercedes and warns at the same time. The goal is not to be liked but to be heard. You are not responsible for how people hear the message. Your only responsibility is *that* they hear it. The Gospel convicts those who are living immoral lifestyles. It's also offensive to those who want God to agree with their out-of-order lives. Gap preachers will put the heat on so-called believers who condone immorality and call it grace. Expect your prayers and voice to be misunderstood by God's people. They turned on Moses when God sent him to free them from Egypt.

Gap men must have the complete love of God in their hearts. You can love God and love His people, and at the same time despise the sin that is cancerously creeping into the Body. The Bible says we are to preach grace *and* truth. Truth sometimes can sound offensive to those who hang their hats on grace only. Suppressing truth is eventually what causes a nation to live without boundaries.

The root of all that we are dealing with concerning sexual immorality, as well as 90 percent of all other challenges we face in society, is that we have forgotten to preach the truth!

I refuse to *only* preach the grace of God. And I refuse to preach *only* truth. To do so would earn me a failing grade on any test. Jesus Himself preached grace *with* truth. As I said earlier, the Church must not preach 50 percent of the message. We must preach 100 percent of God's Word. God says, "If you love Me, you will keep my commands."

Remember, I'm talking to every single person reading this book. We are *all* called to be preachers. Go into all the world and preach the Gospel! And yes, use words. Raise your voice!

One of the greatest signs of the end times is lawlessness. The Bible clearly shows us that the "grace only" preaching we hear today turns a church to lawless living. This sets up a lawless society that eventually turns into a lawless government. It is a global setup for a lawless leader who eventually will look like a savior to the world. We alone will know him as the Antichrist. This ungodly reset is happening as we speak. But God has a reset as well. It will take *gap men* to stand between light and darkness and raise their voice!

Every generation has gap men and women. When you are a gap man, your voice will echo God's Word, not the world you live in. Gap men must have a voice from God that directs the people of God to His heart. Elijah spoke for God and shut up the heavens. The Bible says in James 5 that he prayed earnestly that it would not rain, and it did not rain on the land for three years and six months. Then he prayed again, and the heavens gave rain and the earth produced fruit. All that happened because he stood in the gap of intercession to prove there's only one true God, and His name is Jehovah.

Jeremiah preached the Word, and it was like fire! God spoke to him and said to prepare himself and arise, to speak to the people all He commanded; not to be afraid of their faces but to stand in the

gap and speak on His behalf. Jeremiah was a gap man. He wept
and lifted up the voice of the Lord to the people. He was encouraged by God Himself not to worry about his age or voice, but to
accept the call, regardless.

> Then said I: "Ah, Lord God! Behold, I cannot speak,
> for I am a youth." But the Lord said to me: "Do not say,
> 'I am a youth,' for you shall go to all whom I send you,
> and whatever I command you, you shall speak. Do not
> be afraid of their faces, for I am with you to deliver you,"
> says the Lord. Then the Lord put forth His hand and
> touched my mouth, and the Lord said to me: "Behold,
> I have put My words in your mouth." (Jeremiah 1:6–9)

Whether you are young or old has no merit in the decision.
The enemy will tell you that you are too young, too old. God told
Jeremiah, "Whatever I command you, say it! And don't be afraid of
their faces." God knows that when you stand in the gap, the people
will browbeat you, shoot out their lips, shake their heads, and say,
"Who do you think you are with that self-righteous attitude, telling
us what God is going to do if we don't get right?" Yes, they will.
But keep standing in the gap even if the tomatoes fly, social media
claps back, or you get hateful comments. *Keep raising your voice
with fire* like Jeremiah. It's not your words, it's the Word of God
they are bucking against.

Ezekiel is probably one of the greatest gap men of them all. God
was so emphatic about raising the voices of the watchmen when
they saw the enemy coming that He said spilled blood would be on
their hands if they did *not* raise their voices.

> "But if the watchman sees the sword coming and does not blow the trumpet, and the people are not warned, and the sword comes and takes any person from among them, he is taken away in his iniquity; but his blood I will require at the watchman's hand." (Ezekiel 33:6)

God called Isaiah out as a gap man, directing him to tell the people that if they turned back, God would remove the yoke of tyranny from their necks. Joel, Samuel, Amos, John the Baptist, Peter, Stephen the Martyr, Esther, and others were all gap men. They were unpopular in their moments, but history reveals they were mouthpieces for God. They were trumpet blowers, not just whistleblowers. Chances are you won't be celebrated for standing in the gap until someone writes a book from history's perspective. Keep standing and crying out anyway. Great is your reward in Heaven!

In our society, God is not looking for just one or two people, but hoping that His Church will be filled with *gap men*.

> "If My people who are called by My name will humble themselves, and pray and seek My face, and turn from their wicked ways, then I will hear from heaven, and will forgive their sin and heal their land." (2 Chronicles 7:14)

There will be no change on the earth until the Church humbles itself, lifts up the gap men to intercede, and listens to the Word from Heaven. The beginning of this scripture does not say "when" God's people humble themselves, but "if"!

IF reminds us that it is up to us, not God. IF reminds us that what happens on Earth is not about predestination, but the decisions we make. I've heard it said, "Without man, God will not, but without God, man cannot!"

"If" is always followed with a "then." These are conditional statements. Yes, we serve an unconditional God, but to receive His blessings, God requires action on our behalf. In other words, if we don't, then He won't. If we don't turn from our wicked ways, then He will not hear us from Heaven.

Gap men and women understand that the Kingdom of God is not observation, but participation. In order to see something happen, we've got to get involved. The Kingdom of God is not a place on Earth. It is a positional authority that we speak *from*, not *to*. We don't simply attain it. We operate in it. We are ambassadors, which means we operate from a different standard. Our goal is to raise our voices over the culture and society, and remind people that God is just *and* merciful. But we must remember first that He is *just!*

Plumb lines are standards that are placed during the construction of buildings to keep them straight. If the walls aren't framed according to the plumb line, when the other contractors show up to hang drywall, embellish them with trim, and lay tile, they will be frustrated because the building is out of plumb. The plumb line of the Church is the integrity of God's Word measured against our actions. When an intercessor sees the enemy creeping into God's house and changing the convictions, "evolving" or adding to the Word of God, he must *hold the plumb line!* Gap men will raise their voices to help a church return to foundational truths. The house of God *must be built on the rock*, not the shifting sands of culture.

We need leaders who will hold the line, carry the flag, and incite courage and persistence in others who are fighting alongside them in the middle! As I said, you will need the Holy Spirit to move inside you in order to be a gap man. The Bible says when the enemy comes in like a flood, the Spirit of the Lord raises a standard against it. So when the enemy comes in and tries his best to change the plumb line—seeking to compromise the integrity and convictions of God's people to tolerate sin and even accept it—the gap men must come alive! Get in the middle of the battle and raise the standard. Draw the line!

There is no doubt that we are in a spiritual battle. Hold the line, stand your ground, and don't give the enemy another inch. Ephesians 4:27 says, "Don't give place to the devil." That word, "place," means a foothold! Satan wins by inches, not miles. Just a little at a time; insidious, gradual, and harmful. One spoonful of rejection a day over time eventually leads to depression and then suicide. One spoonful of compromise can cause even the righteous of the righteous to begin a downward spiral into a lukewarm state of mind that becomes a cancer that can spread to others.

What the Church didn't tolerate twenty years ago is now widely accepted. Seventy-six percent of people who go to church now say homosexuality is not a sin. Romans 1:26–32 is the plumb line for this woke ideology concerning the LGBTQ agenda. Not only those who practice it, but those who condone it, are in danger of Hell's flames—even if you're sitting in church weekly.

There's a cold conviction in the Church today. God raises up gap men and gap women. They refuse to embrace wickedness and will expose it so that all can turn from it. The Church at large has embraced what we should be exposing. We need a Church full of gap men who will hold the line concerning conviction and repentance. Paul told Timothy not to back down. Don't water down the truth. Preach, and hold the line.

> This charge I commit to you, son Timothy, according to the prophecies previously made concerning you, that by them you may wage the good warfare, having faith and a good conscience, which some having rejected, concerning the faith have suffered shipwreck, of whom are Hymenaeus and Alexander, whom I delivered to Satan that they may learn not to blaspheme. (1 Timothy 1:18–20)

Paul tells Timothy to hold the line, fight the fight, and wage the good war. It's interesting to me that Paul did not hold back in exposing the names of those who had shipwrecked the faith. He marked people who refused to change their ways. And he did that many times.

He also drops eighteen bombs that will happen in the last days.

> But know this, that in the last days perilous times will come: For men will be lovers of themselves, lovers of money, boasters, proud, blasphemers, disobedient to parents, unthankful, unholy, unloving, unforgiving, slanderers, without self-control, brutal, despisers of good, traitors, headstrong, haughty, lovers of pleasure rather than lovers of God, having a form of godliness but denying its power. And from such people *turn away!* (2 Timothy 3:1–5; emphasis added)

Gap men understand that the last days are full of a great deception, but they will not drop the standard. They will carry the flag in the midst of the battle.

Hold the line! The injustice that is running rampant in our streets needs intercessors. Hold the line! These racist, divisive, and demonic strongholds must come down. Hold the line! The media that celebrate abortion and pedophilia, demanding sympathy for people who rape little children, must be exposed.

Hold the line! The drag queens reading stories to our children in sanctuaries all over the United States of America must be stopped. Intercede and hold the line! While people freely burn Bibles, hold the line! When church reverends are marching in gay pride parades in the name of the Lord, hold the line! When Planned Parenthood sues a church because its members worshiped God outside while babies were being slaughtered inside, hold the line! While so-called worship leaders praise secular music artists who send strong signals of occult practices, hold the line!

The Church is alive and well, but we must storm the gates of Hell. Our voice must be heard in in the middle of the mess. May God raise up *gap men* who will not move from their post or be swayed by the majority!

CHAPTER 10

WHEN VOICES GO MISSING

The Absence of Strong Voices Ushers in Godless Societies

W e have many speakers, but not many *voices*. Most are echo makers. They use a lot of words with a form of godliness, but have no power. Where are voices that hold weight, instill conviction, bring order to a room, and cause us to want to live right? Are they missing—or are they hiding?

Today's world is unique. We are definitely in a culture crisis! The Church is creating a culture, but are we a progressing Kingdom? "Culture" is a huge buzzword in churches everywhere. It indicates the atmosphere, an ecosystem, how we operate, or the feel of the Church. Church houses everywhere are enamored with creating an "environment." Do they understand they can have a large church of confessing Christians who have no access to the Kingdom? The speakers may be popular, but are they truly a voice that God is using? Have they aligned their voices to resonate with the heart of God? Do their voices shift atmospheres, sift out impurity, and separate themselves from the world? Where are those voices?

God is always looking for a voice. Why? Whoever has the ears of His people can direct them. In order to change the future, you have to change the voice. God has a continuing plan to keep a remnant alive on this earth who will not give themselves over to a corrupt and decaying culture. If ever there was a need today, it would be to find fathers and mothers—men and women who fearlessly preach holiness.

Many modern speakers shaping church culture today have led us to believe that the full outcome of Jesus's earthly ministry was grace alone. *That is far from the truth.* Yes, Jesus is our salvation. He is the sacrifice for us to be made holy through His blood. But there is so much more than salvation that He desires for us. The voices who are shaping us must be resolute concerning the Word of God. They must not be prancing, overly polished preachers with no power. I cannot stomach some of the people who have a so-called voice in the Church today. I feel that some of them impress themselves by their mind-boggling flights of fancy. I am fully convinced that many people who speak today need no man to praise them because they have already praised themselves quite sufficiently.

Where are the voices that are not cold concerning sin, Hell, righteousness, godliness, holiness, repentance, and compromise? The glory of God is attached to His holiness. Even the angels pronounce this, and Isaiah caught a glimpse of it. "Holy, holy, holy, the whole earth is filled with His glory," he wrote. Holiness and glory are synonymous. I am looking for the voices that usher in the glory. I believe they are emerging now, but we need a whole army of them! God uses mankind to speak to us. A voice is not limited to a five-fold gospel office. A voice can also be a father, mother, grand-father, grandmother, teacher, political leader, athlete, coach, or more. You can look over your life and point out certain people who made an impact with their voices. How? Typically, they instructed us in right and wrong. They told us how it is or took time to guide us and direct us. God speaks through the voice of mankind. It has always been that way. You are either reading this book because God is verifying your voice or validating the words of others who have a voice in your life.

You can't kill a voice. A voice will resonate inside your head long after the person it belonged to has died. Great and renowned men and women such as Martin Luther King Jr. have shaped the culture we live in today. His voice is still a beacon of light and hope for racial unity in my life. Every year, I ponder his voice, his words, and his influence on our nation. People like Billy Graham, who held crusades across the country and sat with every American president in his lifetime—how powerful his voice was to his generation! But also, great men and women the rest of the world doesn't know and may never find out about have been voices in my life.

When Spiritual Fathers and Mothers Go Missing

I hear this often: "We are not your grandma's church."

What that means is, "We don't do things in an old-fashioned manner. We're up to date." But what was wrong with grandma's church? Isn't that what got most of us here? It was consistent, Bible believing, primitively powerful, and no one cared if you thought it was boring. There were no light shows or LED walls—just a person on the side of the room flipping transparency sheets on an antiquated projector for the congregation to sing the song, or maybe people pulling hardbound hymnals out of the backs of the pews in front of them. There wasn't a huge staff, and the order of service was flip the lights on, worship, preach, issue an altar call, and close. Yet somewhere in that simple age, preachers hammered in conviction.

The words of God that came through the voices that shaped me had that primitive Pentecostal power. My uncle, Pastor Hershel Fee, was my pastor for the first eighteen years of my life. He came to the pulpit ready and passionate! I sat and watched him preach the Gospel, and unbeknownst to both of us at the time, he shaped me with his voice. I found out quickly that the only thing I needed to shape my life was the voice of God coming through a resolute preacher. Everything else was fluff and hype.

What else shaped me? People who weren't concerned if I was offended by God's truth. They were the voice in my life and still are.

I am no longer young. Here is what I see in my forties that I did not see in my thirties: voices who shaped my life beginning to die. They are leaving the earth slowly. Some of them leave suddenly, and some of them gradually. Either way, it hurts to wake up and hear that someone who affected your life tremendously has passed away. Many of them remain voices in my life, but what they have said is all they will say. As I have moved from listening to leading, I have come to realize that though a voice may be gone, its impact remains.

A fleshly body may pass away, but a voice never dies. It simply echoes in the lives that were affected by it. I study the ancient preachers who went on before me. Great preachers preach *from* a place, not *for* a place. I am spiritually attracted to their voices, especially those who were revival-minded.

Some voices are spiritual fathers and mothers I have never met. They lived in a different era, yet they still impact my life. I think of Smith Wigglesworth, Leonard Ravenhill, David Wilkerson, Kathryn Kuhlman, A. A. Allen, Jack Coe, Derek Prince, Myles Munroe (great first name), and others. Some of their voices I have never even heard in recorded form, but I am tremendously shaped by their words!

A voice never dies. It simply leaves you if you don't honor or listen to it.

When Natural Fathers and Mothers Go Missing

My father, Cecil Lee Rutherford, passed away on November 29, 2020. I remember two things about my father's voice: 1. The moment he passed, I didn't want to hear his voice because it triggered such grief in me, and 2. At the same time, I kept thinking, *I will never hear his voice again.*

He had a bolstering voice with a deep thrust. His voice was so low and deep that when I was a child, his just saying my name would strike fear in me. But it also brought affirmation. As I got older, his voice became dear to me and directed me.

One of my father's accomplishments was that he was the official in-store voice of Kmart. At that time, Kmart was larger than Walmart. He was the guy you heard when you were shopping and the announcements would come on over the speakers—in *every* Kmart across the country. He also owned radio stations, satellite companies, and generally enjoyed a lot of success because of his voice.

Toward the end of his life, the greatest influence of his voice was on his family and those who walked closely beside him. Oh God, we need to honor and respect the voices of mothers and fathers in our lives. My living mother, Sue Rutherford, still speaks into my life. Her voice resonates in a softer tone of encouragement. She admonishes and lifts my spirit and my family. God blessed me with parents like these.

The greatest voices missing in the earth today are those of spiritual and natural fathers and mothers. The last verse of the Old Testament rings loudly right now:

> "And he will turn the hearts of the fathers to the children and the hearts of the children to their fathers, lest I come and strike the earth with a curse." (Malachi 4:6)

We need fathers! We need resonant and resolute voices that affirm children, lest a curse come on the earth. Notice also that the Father identifies and affirms Jesus at His baptism, saying, *"This is My son*, with whom I am well pleased." Up to that point, Jesus had done nothing publicly. No dead people raised, no miraculous healings, no prophecies given—yet a Father began speaking to His son and *identifying* Him. This actually gives a level of gravity to Jesus.

It is only at the cross that the voice of the Father leaves Him. "Why have you forsaken Me?" He cried. Why was that? It was the result of Jesus taking on all the feelings of every human so that He could be the High Priest who sympathizes with humanity. He had to experience all pain and emotions. He was beaten, He was spit on, He went through temptations, had people lying about Him and crowds shouting, "Crucify Him!" yet the last emotion was the most unbearable: *"Father, why have You forsaken Me?"*

The last thing Jesus felt before dying on the cross was what it felt like to be fatherless. To not hear the voice of His Father.

We don't hear about any fathers blessing their children until Genesis 9, when Noah blessed two of his three sons and they flourished! But we see fatherly blessing being a big deal that shaped people's destinies throughout the Pentateuch.

What made God tell Abraham to leave his family? He specifically said, "Get away from your father's house so I can bless you!" Abraham's father was supposed to go to Canaan but chose to stop halfway. God told Abraham, "You can't sit here, you have to move. Your father's house has been compromised. The people who listened to your father have stopped moving." God never anoints you for halfway. When you stop, your family stops. We need great men and women to keep raising their voice to move the family forward.

The family is directly affected by the father.

> Moses took his tent and pitched it outside the camp, far from the camp, and called it the tabernacle of meeting. And it came to pass that everyone who sought the LORD went out to the tabernacle of meeting which was outside the camp. So it was, whenever Moses went out to the tabernacle, that all the people rose, and each man stood at his tent door and watched Moses until he had gone into the tabernacle. And it came to pass, when Moses entered the tabernacle, that the pillar of cloud descended and stood at the door of the tabernacle, and the LORD talked with Moses. All the people saw the pillar of cloud standing at the tabernacle door, and all

the people rose and worshiped, each man in his tent
door. (Exodus 33:7–10)

When Moses worshiped, the men worshiped at the doors of
their personal tents. When the father worships at the house, then
his wife and children do, too. We need more fathers in this generation who will set the precedent of worship. As the family goes, so
goes the nation.

This is why it is so vital that the voice of parents cannot go
missing. It is imperative that our lives, our voices, and words as
mothers and fathers shape our children. It's not the government's
job to do this. It's not the schools that should shape our children's
morality. The ones responsible for shaping the next generation are
the mothers and fathers. We need our parents to be the voice of
God in our lives. When a parental voice goes missing, someone
else's voice will take its place.

The first mention of the word "love" in the Bible is not about
the love between a man and woman, but a father and a son—the
story of Abraham and Isaac.

Genesis 22:2 says, "Take your son, whom you love." The voices
that should be the loudest in our lives are that of a father and a
mother who love us.

True love loves you with eternity in mind. The world needs
fathers and mothers right now. You can tell who the true fathers and
mothers are because they are not offended by your lack of acceptance or agreement with what they say; they are only concerned
about your success with God and eternity.

This generation has raised up lovers but not fighters. When a
parent's voice goes missing, you'll find sons and daughters who

will conform to society rather than contend with it. The tough love of a father and a mother keeps us corrected so we don't conform to some ideology that creates confusion later in life. The voices of God-fearing fathers and mothers, spiritual and natural, set us up for success in God and eternity. Their voice establishes boundaries. Paul said this about the generation we are in:

> For the time will come when they will not endure sound doctrine, but according to their own desires, because they have itching ears, they will heap up for themselves teachers. (2 Timothy 4:3)

> For though you might have ten thousand instructors in Christ, yet you do not have many fathers; for in Christ Jesus I have begotten you through the gospel. (1 Corinthians 4:15)

Paul is not speaking against teachers. He is saying there is an absence of a certain kind of voice in your life—the voice of fathers and mothers. A parent's voice does something powerful for you.

When Prophets and Apostles Go Missing

The apostolic voice is a foundational voice. The prophetic voice is a directional voice. I believe these two voices are reemerging right now onto the world scene. They specifically are put in place by God to call people back to foundations and cornerstones. The apostolic ministry does not just raise physical foundations; it reestablishes spiritual foundations. When this voice goes missing, the foundations begin to shake.

> If the foundations are destroyed, what can the righteous
> do? (Psalm 11:3)

The apostolic voice must be reestablished in the Church. The foundations of ministry and yes—most certainly nations—are shaking right now. We have a storm of apostasy going on before our eyes. An apostate church must be confronted by an apostolic ministry! The apostolic ministry carries the blueprint and the divine design to access God's glory. While apostles can operate in the pastoral role, they are not shepherds at heart. They are sent *to set foundations*, to set pillars of truth. When this voice goes missing, so do the foundations. In the New Testament, churches began and grew from this powerful aspect of the fivefold ministry.

We see churches popping up everywhere, but their foundations are weak and unstable. The so-called apostolic voices of today tend to start churches for growth rather than pillars of discipleship. "How big can we get?" cannot be the main thrust of winning people to the Lord. If it is, competition sets in, and that is neither the heart of God nor the heart of a real apostle. The apostle must stay true to foundations. Without the voice of the apostle, true Kingdom expansion fails, and the authority of the Kingdom is replaced with the strategies of man. Prayer is replaced with programs, discipleship in the Word becomes unnecessary, and the people go after whatever entertains them. We need this gift in full operation today—not just the title, but the actual work and the voice of this office.

A prophetic voice not only points to future events but tells us what will happen if we don't turn back to God. Look at the Old Testament. Major and minor prophets all said, "Turn back to God. Here is what happens if you do; here is what happens if you don't!" There aren't shades of gray to a prophetic voice. It's black or white. It's this or that. True prophets are not enamored with money or fame. They typically walk a lonely road of being misunderstood, yet despite this will not accept ungodly vices in God's people.

The voice of God through a prophet is a GPS system. When I put a destination in my phone to direct me, that voice on my phone doesn't care if I am in a conversation, listening to my favorite music, or how famous I am. No, when it's time to make a turn, it's going to interrupt everything else going on in the car. If I don't listen to that voice and I miss my turn, it doesn't stop speaking. It constantly says, "Make a U-turn ahead." That voice will not relent until I personally turn it off. When we come against the prophetic voice, it doesn't stop speaking—but we as a people may have stopped listening.

The prophetic voice is not a point of view. It's a pointing voice! Have you ever watched that TV show, *The View*? Several women, sometimes joined by men, sit around a table discussing current events and giving their different points of view on them. They argue about extremely controversial topics, and nothing really gets resolved. Why? Because America is attracted to reaction, not reality. We have constructed a generation to feed off conflict and call it conversation—but it's actually confusion. This has also happened in the Church. We have too many views and vices, and not enough voices.

We don't need a view. *We need a voice!* Is our voice an actual voice—or is it a vice? Entertainers with valueless voices are bent on giving ad-VICE rather than transmitting God's voice. Ad-VICE is an opinion, not always based on truth but on observation, study, and experience. I'm not saying advice is wrong, but a true prophetic voice does not speak to you out of observation, study, or experience. The prophetic voice is a Spirit-filled voice that speaks on behalf of God, whether His words match the current topography of your life or not. It's not just the voice that tells you, "You're going to get a house on a hill, a brand-new car, millions of dollars coming to you . . ." I'm not against that, but a true prophetic voice turns the hearts of God's people back to Him more than it turns their hearts toward possessions. Possessions don't honor God. The Bible says to honor God with our possessions. The prophetic voices in this past season tainted the office of the ministry by concentrating on wealth and worldly goods. A true prophetic voice points us back to God—money or no money, house or no house.

The prophetic voice came under attack in 2019 and 2020. God deals strongly with the prophet's voice in His Church.

> And the word of the LORD came to me, saying, "Son of man, prophesy against the prophets of Israel who prophesy, and say to those who prophesy out of their own heart, 'Hear the word of the LORD!'"
>
> Thus says the LORD GOD: "Woe to the foolish prophets, who follow their own spirit and have seen nothing!" (Ezekiel 13:1–3)
>
> "My hand will be against the prophets who envision futility and who divine lies; they shall not be in the assembly of My people, nor be written in the record of

the house of Israel, nor shall they enter into the land of Israel." (Ezekiel 13:9)

God is very serious about His prophetic voice on the earth. Matthew Henry's commentary says this about false prophets: "They were not praying prophets; they had no intercourse with heaven; They contrived how to please people not how to do them good."[1] The prophetic voice must first hear from God and must walk in the fear of God. We need the fear of *God* in this office! Right now! Let the prophet's voice rise up and make straight the paths, for Jesus is coming and there isn't much time left.

The Leader's Voice

What happened when the greatest deliverer in the Old Testament went missing? Moses led the people out of Egypt, then went up to hear from the Lord. He spent the next forty days on a mountain receiving instructions and the Ten Commandments to lead God's people. The Bible says in Exodus 20:18 that all the people witnessed the thundering, the flashes, and the mountain smoking where God was, and they trembled. They stood afar off. They told Moses, "You speak with us. If God does, we are going to die." So Moses left them for a season, and they waited for him at the foot of the mountain.

Eleven chapters and forty days later, something happened.

Now when the people saw that Moses delayed coming down from the mountain, the people gathered together to Aaron, and said to him, "Come, make us gods that shall go before us; for as for this Moses, the man who brought us up out of the land of Egypt, we do not know what has become of him." And Aaron said to them, "Break off the golden earrings which are in the ears of your wives, your sons, and your daughters, and bring them to me." So all the people broke off the golden earrings which were in their ears, and brought them to Aaron. And he received the gold from their hand, and he fashioned it with an engraving tool, and made a molded calf. Then they said, "This is your god, O Israel, that brought you out of the land of Egypt!" So when Aaron saw it, he built an altar before it. And Aaron made a proclamation and said, "Tomorrow is a feast to the LORD." Then they rose early on the next day, offered burnt offerings, and brought peace offerings; and the people sat down to eat and drink, and rose up to play. And the Lord said to Moses, "Go, get down! For your people whom you brought out of the land of Egypt have corrupted themselves." (Exodus 32:1–7)

When the voices of great, godly leaders go missing, people rise up unrestrained. The Israelites made their own god, shaped like a cow (Moloch, to be exact—a god to whom children were sacrificed, i.e., abortion).

God was furious. He told Moses to get off the mountain. Joshua met him immediately and said, "There's a sound in the camp. It's not victory. It's not defeat. It's singing." Here is what leaders do when they see God's ways being blasphemed: they come off the mountain, and they are angry. Moses was hot mad! Aaron tried to be a mediator. (Watch out for people who always want to speak for the people and not for God. They're not true leaders. They don't have the heart of God yet if they aren't submissive to His leadership and authority. Stay away from those people!)

Verses 25–26 are powerful:

> Now when Moses saw that the people were unrestrained (for Aaron had not restrained them, to their shame among their enemies), then Moses stood in the entrance of the camp, and said, "Whoever is on the LORD's side—come to me!"

When leaders are not in place, the people will be unrestrained—meaning they have no vision and cast off all restraint so they can do what is right in their own eyes. We need leaders with commanding authority to speak loudly and draw some lines. We must stop doodling and start drawing a line. Raise your voice and make sure people know you are on the Lord's side.

When Men Go Missing

When men call upon the name of the Lord, it changes things. What is happening to our men? They've been targeted for feminization by a feminist movement that says we don't need men. Why is there such an effort to make men effeminate and weak? That comes from a Jezebel spirit of manipulation and control. When men are out of place, society unravels.

There is tremendous pressure on men, and rightfully so. We are built by God to carry a capacity of dominion. When men lust for immorality and turn from truth, we misuse masculinity to go after sensual pleasures, leaving our post of duty and moral obligation. We let someone else rise to the occasion to do our jobs!

We need men. There is a deficit of godly men who will turn from wickedness and go after God. Many men have lost their fight, their drive. They've left the natural order and become soft, effeminate, and homosexual. This is because we misconstrue the natural dominion given to us by God to mean we can operate without accountability. We try to change the Word of God to fit us, but changing the Word does not change the sin.

When voices go missing and do not rise up and communicate the heart of God, the first thing you see in a nation is demoralization. That's when a nation turns aside from good, true, or morally correct ideals. When godly voices go missing or fall silent, we fail to train the next generation and leave it to ungodly educators and others to fill that void. The enemy begins to occupy the young minds of that nation.

You don't change a nation in Congress; you change it in kindergarten.

Demoralization typically takes twelve to fifteen years to solidify roots. After that, even when truth is exposed, the people in a nation will be either unwilling or unable to absorb that truth. The only way to get rid of bad morals is to raise up a new generation. It will take 5 percent of any group to change direction.

After demoralization comes destabilization, when people begin to question everything—such as "Is there such a thing as truth?" "Is the Word of God truth?" "Did God really mean that?" or "What is a woman?"

During destabilization, ungodly voices repetitively speak, looking for those who will agree. It conditions us to accept bad morals. COVID taught us that if you repeat something for long enough, people will stop asking questions and start believing the lies. Then they will ostracize those who continue to question. They say things like, "What's wrong with you?" "You're not complying!" "It's just a shot, and everyone is doing it." See how twisted the Word gets during destabilization? Satan did this in the Garden of Eden. He used the Word to twist the Word.

This will happen to free speech as well if voices don't rise up! When this happens, we are definitely headed toward crisis and a new norm. When a crisis comes, leaders who are already in authority will take that moment to enforce the new norm upon the masses. Could it be that we are being conditioned for a crisis ahead? And if so, where are the leaders who will oppose this? Most importantly, who is speaking on behalf of God? That person, those people, must be in place.

That person is you!

You must not go missing from a future crisis. Raise your voice.

When destabilization happens, or crisis arrives, the remnant of God will be called upon to cry out and prepare God's people to return to His ways. A polarization begins to occur. A strong definition of right and wrong emerges. Preachers will come off the mountain, just like Moses, and draw lines in the sand.

I believe that's where we are today. Voices have been missing for too long. Polarization indicates a sharp, defining contrast, a coming out, a separation of good from evil.

Remnant, raise your voice!

CHAPTER 11

AND MEN LOVED THE DARKNESS

*Ignorance of the Truth Is Not the Problem;
Ignoring the Truth Is!*

It's wild how fast we can adjust from light to darkness. In our house, the lights are on right before we go to bed. I'm able to see and walk around without any problem. The first thing we do after we crawl into bed is flip the lights off. For a moment, it's very dark. It's as if there's no way you're going to see—but then your eyes adjust. Somewhere in the room is a light, perhaps a window that helps illuminate the darkness. Your eye opens its aperture like a camera lens. It can then use that light to see the rest of the room.

Just a few moments earlier, when the lights had just been turned off, there was no way that I would have wanted to get up to walk around. I might have stepped on something or ran into something and possibly hurt myself. However, this wasn't the case after my eyes adjusted. Just a little light—that's all I needed.

To avoid waking my wife, I've often gotten up in the middle of the night and purposefully not flipped on any lights and just gotten around by the light provided—choosing to walk in darkness.

This is a good way to describe why believers choose to walk in darkness: We just don't want to offend anyone. But I am certain that God is offended by the darkness! What about Him?

> In the beginning God created the heavens and the earth. And the earth was without form, and void; and darkness was on the face of the deep. And the Spirit of God was hovering over the face of the waters. Then God said, "Let there be light"; and there was light. And God saw the light, that it was good: and God divided the light from the darkness. God called the light Day, and the darkness he called Night. So the evening and the morning were the first day. (Genesis 1:1–5)

In the beginning God created—but without His voice, nothing had form; the place was void of life, and darkness was the norm. *This is what happens when there is no voice.*

The first thing we see in the Bible is a description of a world in chaos that is confused and feels empty and meaningless. This is where Satan's kingdom thrives on the earth—when things are without form, void, and dark.

Without Form

The Hebrew word for "without form" is *tohoo*. It means "waste, chaos, confusion, desolation, emptiness, meaningless, and worthlessness; total and utter confusion." Does this sound like our world today?

Anywhere man squelches God's voice, order will unravel.

At first, it may feel that we are free from accountability, but that situation moves very quickly into chaos. I believe that this is the order in which Satan works in any area of our lives. In whatever part of life you don't permit the Word of God to enter and hold you accountable, chaos and confusion will eventually result. Here is a quick guide to Satan's method:

1. Turn you away from God's voice by entertaining his (Satan's) voice
2. Get you to turn away from the accountability God's voice provides
3. Decide what we say is better than what God says
4. Operate in our ways instead of God's ways
5. Eat the fruit of our ways and become afraid of God's voice

The result of that process is that the voice of God is no longer comforting to us; it is confronting, and thus to be shunned because it sounds like shame.

You can find this in the beginning when Adam and Eve listened to the voice of the serpent. When we see people living in a world of chaos, without form, we see darkness, gross darkness. We are living in a world of chaos right now. People don't want to see themselves the way God created them. They want to change their sex from male to female and female to male. They want to have sex with animals as well as with children! On February 19, 2023, Spain actually decriminalized sex with animals—saying it's OK as long as the animal is not injured to the point of requiring a visit to the veterinarian afterward.[1]

People who hear the voice of God but don't heed what He says are highly confused about what they are and who they are. They've chosen to listen to voices that are not from God telling them to do whatever they want. They no longer feel accountable to the Word of God. When the only voice they hear is their own—or one that wants them to believe it's their own—such things sound right. Next, you see a community or even a nation embracing such practices. Then, it becomes standard behavior, not even requiring misguided conviction.

Our generation is calling into question the veracity of the Word of God through so-called "deconstruction." "Hath God *really* said?" was one of the first things Satan said to Eve. The major theme of the Satanic church is "Do what thou wilt." Explore, be what you want to be, and be accountable to no one. In this world, we don't call that "being evil," we call it "exploration." We do what we want to do. At first this feels good; however, it always leads to chaos, emptiness, and confusion.

Nobody really pays attention to guardrails on the side of the road until they need them to keep from going over a cliff. When we don't heed the voice of God, it's like passing laws that make the authorities remove the guardrails, then driving on the tops of mountains so we can explore. But the whole purpose of the guardrails is to keep us on the road and away from danger. That's how things work in Satan's kingdom of darkness. He makes us think that a world without accountability, without light, is better than a world with order.

Void

This word also means "empty" or "emptiness." Whenever you stamp the word "void" on something, it means it has to be canceled out and is not usable. Without the voice of God in our lives, we are not only unstable, we are also unusable.

I'm an older man, but every once in a while, for nostalgic purposes, I like to play with those machines where a dollar buys you a chance to move a claw across a sea of stuffed animals. You then position the claw to take a chance at snagging a prize. (It's kind of hard sometimes to pass those things up, even though I don't personally care to *have* a stuffed animal. I guess I like the sense of winning at an activity that seems challenging.) However, every once in a while, I will see a huge sign on the machine that says "out of order." No matter how much money I put in the machine, if it is out of order, I cannot access it.

This is what "void" means. Without the voice of God in our lives, there are certain things we cannot access for any amount of money or skill. Any area of your life to which you have shut the door on God's voice will be "void" of it, and therefore out of order.

Darkness

Chasak is the Hebrew word for "darkness," which means "to withhold light, to be blacked out, death," *and most importantly, "ignorance."* In Genesis, the first thing God spoke into being was light. What was that light? We didn't get the sun and the moon until Day Three. God explains this to us in Isaiah's vision of the angels.

And one cried to another and said:
"Holy, holy, holy is the LORD of hosts;
The whole earth is full of His glory!" (Isaiah 6:3)

The two Hebrew words for glory are *kabod* and *shekinah*. *Kabod* represents the attribute of God; the characteristic of God: *light! Shekinah* represents the embodiment of God; the tangible, seen part of that characteristic. You cannot see the *shekinah* without the *kabod*. The *kabod* is the essence or weightiness of the character of God.

Does light have weight? Albert Einstein said it does. Photons have energy, and Einstein taught us that energy is equal to the mass of a body multiplied by the speed of light, squared. Light has energy, which has mass.

That's deep, but let's break it down. When God said, "Let there be light," it meant that God's Kingdom came to earth. And with that Kingdom came His glory. That's why the angels cried out, "The whole earth is filled with His glory!" His Kingdom is the Kingdom of Light, which is a chief characteristic of God!

John 1:1–4 says:

In the beginning was the Word, and the Word was with God, and the Word was God. He was in the beginning with God. All things were made through Him, and without Him nothing was made that was made. In Him was life, and the life was the light of men.

That word "light" is *phos*. That is where we get the word "photon." It's the manifestation of God, His attributes and His

Kingdom, locked inside of man. The Word of God was the light of man. Jesus calls Himself the Light of the World. He also says *we* are the light of the world in Matthew 5. He is attesting to the fact that we have something in us that shines. People see our good works, and those works glorify the Father in Heaven.

The Kingdom of Light doesn't just work around us—it works in us. Jesus was the embodiment of the Kingdom of Light coming to Earth, according to John 1:14: "The Word became flesh and dwelt among us." He then sat down at the right hand of the Father after His ascension to Heaven. However, Christ—meaning Jesus's attributes and anointing—did not leave the earth. Paul never said that *Jesus* was in us. He said that *Christ* is in us. *And that is the hope of glory for all mankind!*

This is why when Jesus came to Earth, He said, "The Kingdom of God has come." He also said, "The Kingdom of God is within." The Kingdom of God is a manifestation of the glorious light of God that operates in every believer.

Christ, the anointing of Jesus, lies inside us. That light, that Word of God, shines when we are led by the Holy Spirit. Most people know *about* the Holy Spirit. Jesus died for you to know the Holy Spirit. Walking in the power of the Holy Spirit keeps that light burning in our lives. The Holy Spirit transforms our voices, making them resonant and resolute because He fully agrees and aligns with the Word of God.

We can choose to either walk in the flesh or in the Spirit. There are two worlds on this earth. *We live on one Earth, but we can operate in two different worlds*. There is a kingdom of light and there is a kingdom of darkness. The words "light" and "darkness" are interchangeable with two other words: "Light" means knowledge, and "darkness" means ignorance. Even though we live on Earth, that doesn't mean we operate according to the original design God had for us at the beginning. There is another kingdom, and it is a kingdom of darkness. We are either operating in knowledge, or we're functioning in ignorance. Doesn't the Bible specifically say that we are not only destroyed through sin, but that we are also destroyed through our lack of knowledge?

> My people are destroyed for lack of knowledge [of My law, where I reveal My will]. Because you [the priestly nation] have *rejected* knowledge, I will also reject you from being My priest. Since you have forgotten the law of your God, I will also forget your children. (Hosea 4:6 AMP; emphasis added)

Many who read this passage think it says that we just don't know what the truth is. We are ignorant. But that's not what it actually says. It says the people perished because they *rejected* knowledge. *They willfully ignored it!* Who did that? The *priests!* Those who were called to represent the law of the Kingdom of Light thought it best to ignore that light. They cast off all the restraints of God's Word. And because the preachers chose not to restrain sin and sinful behaviors, this affected the next generation. *And men loved the darkness rather than the light.*

John 3:16 is a famous scripture that most people know:

> For God so loved the world that he gave his only begotten son that whosoever believes in him should not perish but have everlasting life.

But what about John 3:19?

> And this is the condemnation, that the light has come
> into the world, and men loved darkness rather than light,
> because their deeds were evil.

It does not say that they liked darkness, or that they were tempted by it. It says they *loved* the darkness. The word condemnation, *krisis*, actually means "decision." And this was the decision the priests made.

The Bible uses very strong language in telling us to have no fellowship with the unfruitful works of darkness but rather to expose them. The word "expose" also means "to rebuke." Speak loudly to the darkness. Raise your voice. Get loud. Nothing changes until somebody raises his voice! Why are we so timid about exposing darkness? Because the men love darkness—and when you stand against it, they will slander you.

The Bible is a light! It exposes darkness. The Bible is the Word of God, and Jesus is the Word and the Light! When we preach the Word, we are preaching light.

Many pulpits today are occupied by light *benders* rather than light *bearers*. They want compromise instead of Calvary, popularity instead of presence, and for too long they've preached for God to agree with them instead of them agreeing with God. Therefore, sin is accepted, love is redefined, murder through abortion is deemed to be okay, drag queens are allowed to preach, and so much more.

Have we lost our values? No—we've lost our light. Many preach psychology rather than salvation!

Isaiah 5:20 says, "Woe to those who call evil good, and good evil; who put darkness for light, and light for darkness."

Isn't it interesting that Nicodemus went to visit Jesus by night because he was afraid to be seen with Him in the light? That would ruin his reputation! Yet that is what *we* do when we seek to keep our reputation and not lose our friends. *We sit quietly in the light, but question God in the dark!*

What happens when the problem is not our ignorance, but that we *choose* to ignore what we know? It's the same as operating in ignorance. Why do we choose to ignore light? Because in darkness there is less responsibility and less accountability. We can gratify our flesh and its desires. This creates chaos in our lives, and yes—it affects others, too. It is possible to fall in love with darkness and actually believe that this only affects us personally. But that is a lie. *We must take full responsibility for the darkness that we, as believers, are not raising our voice against.*

Old Testament prophet Isaiah gives us a prophetic glimpse:

Isaiah 9:2 says, "The people who *walked* in darkness have seen a great light; those who dwelt in the land of the shadow of death, upon them a light has shined" (emphasis added). But when Jesus quotes this in the New Testament, Matthew 4:16 reports that He said, "the people who *sat* in darkness" (emphasis added).

What you walk in, others will sit in! Walking simply means practicing something. Sitting signifies being enthroned on it. *What you practice in one generation, the next generation will live in.*

Between Malachi and Matthew was a period of four hundred years of silence from God. Political battles were taking place and religious sects were forming, including the Sadducees, Pharisees, Herodians, and Essenes. There were religious zealots, legal zealots, political zealots, and separatists. There were four hundred years of darkness because nobody stood in the gap. No one raised his voice for righteousness. Every generation that walked in darkness led to the next generation sitting in it. Then Jesus came into this gross darkness, and a light dawned—and how great was that Light!

God is not offended by darkness, nor is He affected by it. He created light in the middle of darkness. God is not intimidated by it. The smallest amount of light drives darkness out of any room.

Where is that light today? Where is light that is so bright that when people see it, they turn from their darkness? It's in every believer who makes Jesus his or her Lord.

Jesus calls us to be light. He never called us to be a light switch, and He certainly did not call us to be a dimmer. Yet for the sake of not offending people, we tend to flip our switch on and off, or choose to dim our light when we are in certain groups. But God didn't send Jesus to give us a temporary light! He sent the Light of the world into the world so that when we are saved, the Holy Spirit does the work in our hearts. The Holy Spirit is called the Spirit of Truth whom the world cannot receive, but we know Him because He dwells inside us.

If you remove the Holy Spirit, you remove truth. If you remove truth, then why do we congregate at church?

I truly believe that ignorance is not the problem. Ignoring God's ways is 100 percent the mainstream church's issue right now. The world loves darkness, but the Church should love light. It seems to me we have more social clubs and hangouts then we do churches. They just happen to meet under the name "church."

Ignorance means to not *know* something; ignoring means to *refuse* to know it.

Ignorance is about not *having* the information; ignoring is about having the information, but not *using* it.

Our challenge as the Body of Christ is not ignorance, it's the practice of ignoring truth. Darkness crept in and looked good. We need the sledgehammer of truth to break open the nasty, vulgar love of the world that has made God's people follow darkness rather than light!

People have suppressed truth. Suppressing the truth leads to oppressing the righteous. Romans 1 speaks strongly of the sexual sins and deviances that we are seeing in our culture today, and the warning given to the Roman church is just as applicable to us.

> For the wrath of God is revealed from heaven against all ungodliness and unrighteousness of men, who suppress the truth in unrighteousness, because what may be known of God is manifest in them, for God has shown it to them. For since the creation of the world His invisible attributes are clearly seen, being understood by the things that are made, even His eternal power and Godhead, so that they are without excuse, because, although they knew God, they did not glorify Him as God, nor were thankful, but became futile in their thoughts, and their foolish hearts were darkened....
>
> Therefore God also gave them up to uncleanness, in the lusts of their hearts, to dishonor their bodies among themselves, who exchanged the truth of God for the lie, and worshiped and served the creature rather than the Creator, who is blessed forever. Amen.

For this reason God gave them up to vile passions. For even their women exchanged the natural use for what is against nature. Likewise also the men, leaving the natural use of the woman, burned in their lust for one another, men with men committing what is shameful, and receiving in themselves the penalty of their error which was due.

And even as they did not like to retain God in their knowledge, God gave them over to a debased mind, to do those things which are not fitting; being filled with all unrighteousness, sexual immorality, wicked-ness, covetousness, maliciousness; full of envy, murder, strife, deceit, evil-mindedness; they are whisperers, back-biters, haters of God, violent, proud, boasters, inven-tors of evil things, disobedient to parents, undiscerning, untrustworthy, unloving, unforgiving, unmerciful; who, knowing the righteous judgment of God, that those who practice such things are deserving of death, not only do the same but also approve of those who practice them. (Romans 1:18–32)

This all started because people who knew better suppressed the truth. It means they held it back. The next thing you see is God giving them over to sexual uncleanness, fornication, porn, lust, etc. *They exchanged the truth of God for a lie.* This isn't just about homosexuality; this is about sexual perversion of all kinds outside of the confines of God's creative order.

We see that God gives them up to these vile passions. This is where homosexuality begins. Homosexuality is a symptom of a problem, not the source. What is the source? People who've suppressed the truth—God's people! Those who know better! And then finally, you see that after God gives them over, there is a downward spiral of their minds to do other things which are not fitting. They invent even more evil things.

What in the world have we yet to see when darkness has been set loose and nobody raises his voice for the sake of truth? Don't think that just because you merely condone homosexuality instead of practicing it that you are safe. No, Paul says that those who approve of the practice will see death.

Where is the fear of God? Where in the world did we go wrong? The world has gone wrong because we became a generation that questioned the truth rather than a generation that stands for it!

Why is truth so often questioned in our generation? The objective truth, the Word of God, the truth for everyone whether we agree or not, is now being called subjective truth—meaning, *my version.*

Jesus tells us in John 17 that we sanctify ourselves in truth, and He defines what truth is. It's the Word of God.

> "Sanctify them by Your truth. Your word is truth. As You sent Me into the world, I also have sent them into the world. And for their sakes I sanctify Myself, that they also may be sanctified by the truth." (John 17:17–19)

This means that when we separate and sanctify ourselves, it affects everyone around us—just as others are affected when we don't. Our choices affect everyone around us. Our suppression of truth has created heterosexual immorality, dishonor, sexual revolution, rampant pornography, homosexuality, and a downward moral spiral to the point that the Church is now embracing what we are called to expose. We must get back to raising our voices for the truth for the sake of exposing the darkness. Stop loving the darkness and start living in the light! Expose the darkness, no matter the cost.

CHAPTER 12

THEY/THEM

Satan's Agenda Is Not Only about Identity

We need a revival of sanity and moral proclivity. The world has gotten ludicrous concerning sexual identity. This has created deep and widespread deviancy. Satan's agenda to change our God-given identity is in full effect. However, this is not the end goal for the spiritual wickedness pushing this agenda. Something deeper is evolving, something more gravely concerning than even the obvious attack on identity.

Something new has emerged in the culture today: the use of pronouns as an identifying force separate from one's sex at birth. According to some, you can identify yourself however you want. If you want to change your definition of sex from male to female, you can say *he/she*. Want to be more than that? You can be *they/them*. People who identify outside of their God-given gender at birth are allowed to use nongendered or nonbinary pronouns.

This demonically driven, gender-neutral inclusivity is extremely deceptive and has a deeper goal that boils down to this: genitalia does not equal gender. Many of our governmental leaders have embraced this ideology as truth. Some have gone as far as to offer sex changes to children even without parental consent, claiming the parent is causing "psychological damage" to children who want to change their sex while those children are just innocently exploring their God-given identities.[1] They say sex is what you were born with, and gender is fluid. They say gender has to do with how you feel and wish to express yourself to others. Pathological lying has risen to the national level. Somewhere between conscious deception and delusion, the world has bought into this subjectivity. The greatest strategy to make a lie seem like truth is to embed it in something that is actually true.

In the last days, there will be a great deception.

> For the mystery of lawlessness is already at work; only He who now restrains will do so until He is taken out of the way. And then the lawless one will be revealed, whom the Lord will consume with the breath of His mouth and destroy with the brightness of His coming. The coming of the lawless one is according to the working of Satan, with all power, signs, and lying wonders, and with all unrighteous deception among those who perish, because they did not receive the love of the truth, that they might be saved. And for this reason, God will send them strong delusion, that they should believe the lie, that they all may be condemned who did not believe the truth but had pleasure in unrighteousness. (2 Thessalonians 2:7–12)

One of the greatest deceptions of our days comes straight from the heart of the leaders of the LGBTQ movement. Why do we continue to believe this lie? Because rejecting information means you have to do research to back up your statement, and it's easier to simply accept what we're told. We'd rather believe the lie than take the time to collect the information needed to disprove it. Therefore, we remain silent and tolerant. Whether we actually agree or not, our silence says we do. That is why the devil is working so hard: He sees a door of opportunity to confuse the masses about their God-given identity, and thereby steal their God-given authority.

Something even more delusional than this is coming. Satan's end game is to not only change your identity, he wants your authority!

If you have not been given authority to do something, you cannot use it. But it's also possible to have authority and not know how to use it because you don't understand your identity—and that's what all this gender confusion is ultimately about.

Let me explain.

Genders and Pronouns

While watching TV one day a few years ago, I saw, to my surprise, that our state college was on the national news. Kennesaw State University in Kennesaw, Georgia, had created an official document stating we should be sensitive to gender neutrality and that our language needs to drive that change through pronouns. The university's LGBTQ Resource Center released a pamphlet offering guidance on gender neutral pronouns. Though the list is ever evolving, here is the most recent version I could find:

He/She/They/Ne/Ve/Ey/Ze/Hir/Ze/Zir/Xe/They/Them...
There are even pronouns out now that say you can be called "demon."[2]

It's no coincidence that those already confused by sexual identity, the LGBTQ+, are the voices seeking to bring about this change.

Psychologists and sex experts have come up with some very interesting definitions of gender identity:

1. Cisgender: the person allows their genitalia at birth
    to determine their gender.

2. Transgender: the person's genitalia at birth does not
    match the gender with which they identify.

3. Nonbinary: the person does not identify as either
    male or female.

4. Intersex: the person was born with both male and
    female genitalia.

5. Genderqueer or bi-gender: the person identifies as
    both male and female.

6. Gender-fluid: the person allows their feelings to dic-
    tate their gender expression at any given moment.
    (Male today, female tomorrow, etc.)

7. Gender nonconforming or omni-gender: the person
    adopts an attitude that says they are free of any gender
    norms regardless of how they identify. For example, a
    biological male may choose to wear makeup or nail
    polish that is typical for women but seeks to be called
    by some pronoun that is neither male nor female.

8. Gender expansive: the person takes an "anything
    goes" approach to their gender identity and expression.

For example: "I identify as a panda-demon-bird they/them."

9.　Pangender: all genders at once.

10.　Two-spirit: the person adopts an attitude that says, "I identify with a third gender that encompasses both a masculine and feminine spirit. I have two spirits in me."

Did you notice that among all those options, "male" and "female" didn't even make the list? It continues to grow and so does the number of demon-possessed youth we are seeing today.

Satan's End Game with This Mass Deception

So what is this all about, really? The enemy's ultimate deception is to remove authority, not just identity.

Authority comes from identity. When you remove identity, you remove authority. This is why you pull over when an officer in uniform flags you down. If anyone else tried to do that, you would just ignore them. But because the officer's identity is not in question, neither is his authority to pull you over. The badge on his chest clearly identifies who he is. If, for whatever reason, you decide to deny his identity and the authority that goes with it, you will be meeting with other officers in his precinct shortly thereafter! The badge says: "If you mess with my authority, I have backup."

The officer has full authority to use his weapons in the event that you challenge him. He also has the authority and power to disarm you.

Anytime you see the enemy confusing identity, you will see that authority is the next thing he will strip from a nation or person.

Let me explain this with scripture:

> Now when the tempter came to Him, he said, "If You are the Son of God, command that these stones become bread."
>
> But He answered and said, "It is written, 'Man shall not live by bread alone, but by every word that proceeds from the mouth of God.'"
>
> Then the devil took Him up into the holy city, set Him on the pinnacle of the temple, and said to Him, "If You are the Son of God, throw Yourself down. For it is written: 'He shall give His angels charge over you,' and 'In their hands they shall bear you up, lest you dash your foot against a stone.'"
>
> Jesus said to him, "It is written again, 'You shall not tempt the LORD your God.'"
>
> Again, the devil took Him up on an exceedingly high mountain, and showed Him all the kingdoms of the world and their glory. And he said to Him, "All these things I will give You if You will fall down and worship me."
>
> Then Jesus said to him, "Away with you, Satan! For it is written, 'You shall worship the LORD your God, and Him only you shall serve.'"
>
> Then the devil left Him, and behold, angels came and ministered to Him. (Matthew 4:3–11)

Look at the pattern. Right before Jesus is revealed as the great-est deliverer in all of history, a deceiver comes. Deceiving voices come *before* deliverance voices. *As Jesus is about to raise His voice to His generation, waiting to fulfill what He was called to do on this earth, the enemy moved in.*

The first temptation of Jesus does not really concern hunger; its root is in identity. "*If* you are the Son of God." Because Jesus was human as well as God, Satan called His "sonship" into question. Jesus responded with "It is written." The second temptation also shows the devil questioning His identity, and again Jesus responds by saying, "It is written." But on the third temptation, Satan does not question His identity; he wants Jesus to relinquish His authority. This is where the Body of Christ is right now. Satan said to Jesus, "Bow down and worship me, and I will give all of this to you!"

This is where Jesus inserted His human emotion. He did not start with, "It is written"—He came back with attitude: "*Away with you, Satan!*" When Jesus's authority was questioned, He met Satan with a bolstering and emotionally charged authoritative response! *Get out!* This should also be the response of the Church of Jesus upon the earth today as our children are being maimed for life! It is straight mutilation of their identity: Cut off the sperm that *produces* the next generation and cut off the breasts that *provide* for the next generation. It is sickening what the devil is feeding our society.

But what is more sickening is the silence from the Church. Our silence speaks so loudly that it's deafening. We must raise our voice on this matter for the sake of our children. Jesus's response should be ours as well: "*Get out, Satan!*" And we should say it with *attitude!*

The sin that has entered individuals through trauma, molestation, or something else that happened to them at a young age is now being taught in our educational systems and legislated by our governmental bodies. The Bible specifically says the way we treat ourselves is how we will treat others. My greatest concern is that we have a generation that encourages such lifestyles because of their own trauma, then teaching another generation that hasn't experienced trauma that this is God's way. Trauma is not the reason people turn to homosexuality anymore. Now it's teaching that says, "I'm like this. It's okay if you want to be, too."

I refuse to accept this. Gender is not fluid. The Word of God hasn't "evolved." Even Jesus said He created humans as male or female. There aren't any "they/them"! If you have a penis, you are male. You are a man. If you have a vagina, you're female. You are a woman. It is as simple as that, and it's been like that since the beginning of creation.

There's only one place in the Bible that refers to a "they/them": The demon-possessed man who met Jesus on the shores of Gadara and said, "I am Legion, for we are many." I prophesy this demonic, agenda-driven spirit will be cast off this generation and nation! You can't have our children! Church, raise your voice on this subject. What we allow in the classroom in one generation will lead Congress in the next. Don't be quiet.

Get an attitude just like Jesus. The greatest threat to our society is not bombs, guns, or electromagnetic pulses, it's a Church that refuses to raise her voice. Raise your voice right in the middle of this satanically charged attack. Speak up. This is about your authority. You will come under fire. Be resolute, do everything you can, and having done all...*stand!* Don't bow on this.

The kingdom of darkness is not affected by whether you belong to a church or even believe in Jesus. The Bible says even demons believe, so what separates us from them? We have been given authority in the name of the Lord Jesus Christ, and Satan and his demons don't want you to use it. Your church attendance, social hangouts, or weekly hour of feel-good sermons do not weaponize you as a believer. Only one thing does: the authority given to us by our identity as God's sons and daughters.

Identity and Authority

Americans all have nine numbers attached to them. They are called Social Security numbers—our government-given identities. Without them, we cannot access many things. But in the Kingdom, our identity is found in one word: Jesus. That name fills you with authority! Get used to using it. When two or three agree, asking anything in His name, it can be done. God has given us the name of Jesus, with His full power and authority on Heaven and Earth. Your identity is you in Christ, but your authority is Christ in you.

The Bible says, "Christ is in you, which is the hope of glory." The actual glory of God is inside every believer who walks in the ways of Jesus Christ. You're no threat to the enemy if you're quiet about your faith. Get an attitude—you have authority!

The difference between identity and authority is as simple as this: When you go to a hotel, they give you a key card to your room with the name of the hotel on it. But your door does not open because it has the hotel name on it; it opens only after you pay for the room and the hotel staff electronically infuses the card with a magnetized code. That code tells the door it has to open. The Holy Spirit inside you is the magnetized code that makes doors open!

Heaven knows your name when you get saved. Hell knows your name when you get baptized in the Holy Spirit. Doors have to open, and demons have to listen. You walk in a powerful authority, and your voice activates it!

Love and Acceptance—or Love and Repentance?

When sexual sin is endorsed at the highest levels of government, God will deal with that nation. He will raise voices up that will not respect that which is defined outside of the Word of God. And He will deal with His house first. Those who minister before the Lord and condone sexual deviance and deception in the House of God—ordinating perverted people and raising symbolic rainbow flags to honor immoral behavior—will be dealt with. But when you confront evil in high places, you will be blessed, as King Amaziah was (see 2 Chronicles 25).

This is not hate speech; this is the Word of the Lord. This "love yourself, define-yourself" society is a slap in God's face. Love is not love; *God is love.* God's Word doesn't call for love and acceptance. It calls for love and repentance. When we experience the love of God, something should change inside us.

You don't just get saved, you get delivered. Our generation and our children's deserve to know the truth—not their truth, *the* truth. My wife often says from the pulpit, "They deserve to be free!" It's not truth that sets you free, it's *knowing* the truth and walking in it.

Whichever kingdom wins the hearts of this next generation will bless or curse the next twenty years of our lives.

I believe that every devil in hell that has exercised influence on this generation concerning their identity, and authority is coming down. *We must move this generation from transgender ideology to transformed ideology.* Never before have I felt God sending so many to prepare for something so quickly. The enemy knows his time is short and he must confuse a generation so they cannot rise up in authority. It's not hate speech to warn people when you know they are going straight to Hell while culture, and even some church people, celebrate. Saying nothing is actually hate! Remaining silent is to not show the love of Jesus Christ.

How did this sin take over the nations, get into our government, change the definition of marriage, and ostracize the voice of God by calling it hate speech? Because we forgot who we were and gave up our authority by bowing to the demonic demands of a people bent on refusing truth. We surrendered to a godless culture. We began to take our cues from something other than the Word of God. We *suppressed truth.* Then we slowly caved and compromised our morals to fit in and not stand out. All it took was a small drop of the knee from God's people in order to conform to the demonically driven LGBTQ agenda.

We gave Satan a foothold. One inch at a time, we tolerated this sin as it moved from the individuals coming out of the closet, to partnering with local alliances, to communities being taken over, to corporations sponsoring such ridiculousness. Then it moved to the federal level when the White House, the most iconic house in the nation, was lit up with the colors of the rainbow to celebrate homosexuality. And we sit in silence? We say nothing because we're afraid to be called "insensitive"?

How do we turn this tide? Speak the truth and let it draw a line in the hearts of the people! Jude 1:22–23 says,

And on some have compassion, making a distinction; but
others save with fear, pulling them out of the fire, hating
even the garment defiled by the flesh.

Sign of the Times

"I just can't go to church anymore. It's just a bunch of hell, fire,
and brimstone." I wonder if that's what people said right before
Sodom and Gomorrah were destroyed. *We need people who will
raise their voices regardless of whether sinners get saved or not.
We need them to warn us.* That's what Noah did, and God praised
him for it! We must start preaching so strongly that it pulls people
out of the fire in which their feet are firmly fixed. All across this
nation, those following the LGBTQ agenda are teaching the massive deception that God has blessed their scheme. This lie must be
met with a deliverer. *A voice.*

The Bible says the last days will be like the time of Sodom and
Gomorrah and the days of Noah. What's the sign of Noah's time?
A rainbow. What was the dominant sin of Sodom and Gomorrah?
Sexual deviancy! What is the deception? "It's all about love." No!
This lie is perversion in God's eyes. It has gotten to such a level
today that some even openly propose that Jesus was gay. Where are
Satan's biggest supporters in this? Some go to church.

*Good and evil have grown a tree right inside the courts of our
church houses, and a generation is eating the fruit of our silence.*
Stop! Stop! Stop agreeing and saying we are for it, that it's okay.
No, it's not okay! And the Church needs to say it's not okay. It's
blasphemous. It's not the people we need to rise against, it's the

spirit in and behind this agenda. I rebuke this demonic spirit that has been unleashed.

Church, we're not called to sit back and say, "Well they will get what they deserve." No, God is looking for trumpet blowers who will stand up and say, "This is not right!" *This* is the way, walk in the ways of the Lord." We must stop playing church and start being a voice to our society, even if it's the last message people ever hear from us.

I prophesy that an LGBTQ revival is coming. When people get free from this spirit of perversion and confusion, they are going to light the kingdom of darkness on fire. But until that happens, we cannot affirm this lifestyle and call ourselves believers. It is against Scripture to do so.

> [W]ho, knowing the righteous judgment of God, that those who practice such things are deserving of death, not only do the same but also approve of those who practice them. (Romans 1:32)

We must raise our voice on this issue.

CHAPTER 13

LOUD AT 11

Get Louder than "Hell"

In late 2017, the Spirit of God told me and my wife to have the church we pastor pray in the Holy Ghost for fifteen minutes every morning for an entire month. *Don't question it, just do it,* He said.

We shared this with our church. For the next thirty days, we woke up in the morning and spent fifteen minutes praying in the Holy Spirit. After thirty days, I thought, *What was that all about?*

The next Sunday, we held our annual Christmas Evening service. Worship with Wonders Church is not a suit-and-tie kind of place, but that day we said, "It's a special occasion, let's get dressed up and wear our Christmas best." Although we are a very Spirit-filled and Spirit-led church, we knew this night would be more traditional and orthodox. We would do the programmatic cantata-style service in which each ministry of the arts would be present.

As we began to close the service, a demon-possessed woman approached the right side of the stage. My wife jumped off the stage with Holy Ghost authority and began to deliver the woman. At the same time, the ushers were waving from the back left corner of the sanctuary to get over there because a man had dropped dead! As we pushed through the crowd to get to him, I heard everyone in the church praying in the Holy Spirit.

I saw the lifeless man; his eyes were glazed, his mouth was open, and our emergency team was standing over him, compressing his chest almost to the point of breaking bones. They brought out a defibrillator and began yelling, "Three, two, one, shock!" The words on the screen said, "No pulse."

But something was stirring. For the first time in my life, I could see death but could not feel it in the room.

The EMTs stopped what they were doing, and we put our hands underneath the man's head and yelled, "Holy Spirit, breathe!" With no compressions or shocks, the man gasped for breath! This happened not because of paddles or compression. Those had been tried. It happened because of people praying.

Later that week, our emergency team leader called my wife and casually mentioned that the man had been dead for fifteen minutes before we laid hands on him. My wife and I were shaken. God had just asked for us, as a church, to pray in the Spirit for fifteen minutes a day for a month. Then a man died in our church service for exactly fifteen minutes.

When an emergency strikes, we are taught to call 911. Immediately, the city will dispatch an ambulance to get to you. If the need is great, if there is no life in the body, the EMTs will violently rip the clothes off your chest, speak strongly to those around you to get away, and then proceed to shock your body. No one questions them because they have been sent to do whatever it takes to save your life. As a last resort, they will take out paddles and shock your body!

This is what eleventh-hour voices do. Theirs are like the voice of John the Baptist. When they speak, they shock the Body. *Eleventh-hour voices are not concerned about offending the Body.* They recognize that their mission involves inconveniencing others to interrupt the ongoing program.

If you're waiting on God to work through you on *your* schedule, hang it up! This is where God separates the interested and the invested. Eleventh-hour Christians are hungry for revival, no matter what the cost or what others think. They are ready to receive the harvest, shock dead bodies, and watch God move.

America and the nations are about to be *shocked* at what God will do in this eleventh hour. But it will take voices to shift from idle position and into gear.

> "And about the eleventh hour he went out and found others standing idle, and said to them, 'Why have you been standing here idle all day?' They said to him, 'Because no one hired us.' He said to them, 'You also go into the vineyard.'" (Matthew 20:6–7)

Preacher, I want to ask you the same thing God once asked me: What would you preach about if you knew it was the last time people would hear you? Money? Successful living? Psychology? How to have better sex with your spouse? (Yes, that is a thing in the pulpits.) Would you entice them with secular antics or secular music in order to be cool and hip, or would you preach repentance, holiness, revival, the fear of God, and a message that would bring conviction to their bones? God told me, "Preach like that! *Preach like it's the last time they will ever hear you.*" Get loud!

The Remnant Must Get Louder than Hell

Hell is in our streets, classrooms, families, churches, cities, and government. The devil is neither hiding nor silent. God is raising up voices—including yours—to boldly proclaim in this last hour, "Prepare the way of the Lord!"

There is a Bible story that talks about the ending of a day and the coming of night. Just before the day closes, a landowner hires a group of people at the eleventh hour (5:00 p.m.). The implication is that the harvest is great. More laborers are needed, and here is a group of people who can get it done. These people just need to have a place for their voices to speak, their sickle to swipe, and the harvest to be reaped!

The "eleven" has meaning. We are in the world's eleventh hour. *We are in the last seconds of the last days*. The eleventh hour means you're one hour away from midnight—the end of time, the end of the game. God is giving the Church one more chance to get it together, to bring the harvest in. Our children will eat the fruit of what we decide to do in this uncomfortable season.

The number eleven also has a biblical meaning.

- Daniel sees ten horns and then one more, which is eleven. The eleventh horn is the Antichrist.
- Genesis 11 is the chapter about the tower of Babel— mankind's rebellion with intent to become God themselves.

- Eleven kings from Genesis to Revelation were offended by Truth.

"Eleven" represents a time when lawlessness is praised, truth is questioned, and Jesus is mocked. How many artists, world leaders, and social media influencers have we seen mocking Jesus lately? *Satan is being praised, and Jesus is being mocked.* It represents irresponsibility, lawlessness, disorder, chaos, judgment, and rebellion. Everything gets turned upside down, and good and evil seemingly switch places. It is during the eleventh hour that God will raise up radical voices who can accomplish in one hour what others couldn't accomplish in an entire day!

The eleventh hour represents a generation of formerly idle believers whom God employs. They have been in the marketplace all day and awake, but not active. Other believers in the field will be offended by eleventh-hour Christians who not only carry the identity of Jesus Christ, but the authority of Jesus Christ. They walk heavily with authority, boldness, and power—a strength that gets the harvest in. Don't judge who God will use by what they look like, what they wear, or where they came from. They will not be politically correct. The voice of the remnant will be staggeringly bold.

We are in the eleventh hour. This parable speaks of how the Jews were called first, then the Gentiles. We are all able to work the field so long as we stop standing idly by when God calls us! Idle simply means the engine is on and the power is there, but the car is not moving. God is calling you to SHIFT: Seed Hitting In Fertile Timing. The time is now, and the seed is the Word of God. When you shift a car, it means you have reached the full capacity of the gear you are currently in and must transition to the next gear to move farther, faster. Transition is when you don't know enough to go forward but you know enough not to go backward. Eleventh-hour Christians are shifting the Body of Christ.

In 2 Timothy 3, Paul writes that in the last days, there will be people who have a form of godliness but deny its power. *Perilous times call for a powerful Church.* We cannot afford to be inactive. Everyone is crying out for a revival and an awakening, but that means God has to intervene.

The awakening is here. Some preachers may disagree with me that the awakening has not started—but it has! We are in the conditioning phase. The world is doing its best through systematic crisis, planned political pawning, mandates, masks, and gaslighting to see how far you will go along with its agenda. Yes, we have been awakened, but a voice must arise! *Get up and get loud.*

Hell is doing its best to get louder than the Church. Satan's role in the last days is simple: *Have people embrace lawlessness.* Have them accept abortion. Tell them to deconstruct their faith, question their existence, alter their identity, and explore the soft side of rebellion. We have changed the names of sin to adult entertainment, minor-attracted people, sex education, and marriage equality.

No, it's sin! No matter how the devil redefines it, it's sin. And the Church must get loud! Our silence is deafening.

Raise Your Voice in Praise

Remember Paul and Silas? The Bible says they were being kept in a secure dungeon, with their feet and hands fastened in chains. They had been severely beaten and thrown into jail, then moved to the inner dungeon. The jailer was commanded to keep them under watch. What a threat to the kingdom of darkness they must have been!

Just before midnight, they chose to sing. The Bible says they were singing so loud that the other prisoners heard them. And then suddenly, the earth shook, the chains were loosed, and *all* the prisoners were set free. My good friend, Pastor Tony Suarez, says that what you do at 11:59 p.m. determines what you will get at midnight. Eleventh-hour Christians are prevailing praisers.

Psalm 149 says, "Let the high praises of God be in their mouth!" The proper translation of the word used is "throat." That means the praises of eleventh-hour Christians come from their spirits, not their lips. God is bringing back the power of a people who call out to Him. I hear the sound of praise bellowing out in eleventh-hour voices. Raise your voice with praise to God.

For too long, we have had a limited view and conception of praise. It's not the first two songs performed in a service to get us hyped. Praise is the response to something we value. True praise is not an emotional reaction, but a proactive declaration. We praise in every condition, not just because we feel inspired. Do you realize what praise will do in your situation or in the nation?

Eleventh-hour voices are bringing people back to praise the name of the Lord. Something happens when we corporately praise God together. Praise summons the Presence of God right in the middle of our circumstances. The Word of God says, "He inhabits the praises of His people." If we want God in our nation, we must lift up our voices and praise. Turn our weeping into worship. Turn our pain into praise.

God, help us in this eleventh hour to focus more on bringing glory to You rather than ourselves!

Praise brings the glory! Second Chronicles 5:13 says that when the people lifted up their voices with the trumpets, the glory of God fell in the room. Notice the word "lifted." They got loud. You desire to see the glory in your generation? Praise loudly. The glory of God fell so strongly that the priests could not even stand because of the glory cloud of God.

Second Chronicles 20 speaks of a king named Jehoshaphat who was surrounded by three armies. He prayed to God for deliverance. The Bible says he surrounded himself with Judah's camp. Judah is synonymous with praise. God tells him that He will fight the battle. Jehoshaphat tells the army that if God is going to do this, to send out the praisers first. He placed the most skilled warriors, warriors who would normally take the front line, in the back. He raised up the praisers and said, "Lead the charge!" and the enemy was destroyed. Don't tell me not to get loud! Our praise must be exuberant. Louder than hell!

True praise is not hindered by pride. David danced before the Lord with all his might. He stripped himself of any kingly authority as he brought the Ark of the Covenant—the presence of God—back into the nation. He danced before the Lord. His wife peered out the window and detested his praise. When David reached the door of his house, she mocked him. David's response was the response of eleventh-hour praisers today: "If you think I am undignified now, wait until God shows up again. I will be even more undignified than this!"

Eleventh-hour Christians are loud believers who don't care who else is in the battle or who's in the prison. Their praise, their worship, and their commitment to God will not be silenced by cancel culture or comfortable Christianity. They want change, and they want it now. The harvest is ripe.

You are not called to be quiet. Pentecost ignited a voice! In Acts 2, the Church was born after the Holy Spirit fell. One hundred twenty people gathered in an upper room, and the next thing you see is Peter standing up and raising his voice. *Getting loud!* If God didn't want you to say anything, you would have been born without a voice. You are anointed for the eleventh hour.

Eleventh-hour voices are loud in the prayer room. The Church must move away from massive passivity concerning the prayer room. If we truly want revival, prayer services will be bigger than our Sunday morning services.

There's a call for eleventh-hour voices. Let them speak. They have a harvest in mind.

CHAPTER 14

SECOND WIND

How God Uses Our Voice to Bring Revival

Read this chapter out loud. It'll put a fresh wind of the Spirit of God on you!

The LORD took hold of me, and I was carried away by the Spirit of the LORD to a valley filled with bones. He led me all around among the bones that covered the valley floor. They were scattered everywhere across the ground and were completely dried out. Then he asked me, "Son of man, can these bones become living people again?"

"O Sovereign LORD," I replied, "you alone know the answer to that."

Then he said to me, "Speak a prophetic message to these bones and say, 'Dry bones, listen to the word of the

LORD! This is what the Sovereign LORD says: Look! I am going to put breath into you and make you live again! I will put flesh and muscles on you and cover you with skin. I will put breath into you, and you will come to life. Then you will know that I am the LORD.'"

So I spoke this message, just as he told me. Suddenly as I spoke, there was a rattling noise all across the valley. The bones of each body came together and attached themselves as complete skeletons. Then as I watched, muscles and flesh formed over the bones. Then skin formed to cover their bodies, but they still had no breath in them.

Then he said to me, "Speak a prophetic message to the winds, son of man. Speak a prophetic message and say, 'This is what the Sovereign LORD says: Come, O breath, from the four winds! Breathe into these dead bodies so they may live again.'"

So I spoke the message as he commanded me, and breath came into their bodies. They all came to life and stood up on their feet—a great army. (Ezekiel 37:1–10 NLT)

A fresh wind is coming. It's here! Powerful prophetic voices from around the globe will release a *ruach* from God upon the Church. The dead, stale, dry bones from the last season will come alive and become militant. After every shaking, shifting, and sifting, there is a gathering of what "remains." Don't cry over what has been lost, look around at who remains! Look around at what is left, and watch what God will do.

If you're on this earth, you carry the breath of God, and you have purpose. If you're here, it's because *you* remain. Revelation calls us to strengthen what remains.

> "Wake up, and strengthen and reaffirm what remains [of your faithful commitment to me], which is about to die; For I have not found [any of] your deeds completed in the sight of my God or meeting his requirements." (Revelation 3:2 AMP)

Wake up! Those words are only said when someone is sleeping. I firmly believe that those words have already been spoken in our current season. It's not a matter of waking up—the Great Awakening is upon us—but we in the Church are groggy, sleepy-eyed, a bit brain-fogged, and right now it's a matter of getting up and speaking up.

The cultural phrase "woke" must be met by a militant Church that is awake. What do we do when we wake up? Strengthen what remains. God is coming upon His people with the spirit of might. "Be strong, be of good courage and go forth!"

I want to preach to you something you need to know right now: You are going to get your wind back!

> Therefore, strengthen the hands which hang down, and the feeble knees. (Hebrews 12:12)

Take a new grip on the sword of the spirit. In this new season, we—the remnant of God—are fighting differently. Our voice is a clapback that makes a comeback. Jim Raley, pastor of Calvary

Church in Ormond Beach, Florida, says, "Our revenge will be revival!" That ministry God gave you is not dead. That calling on your life is not dead, and that voice you have been given is not to be silenced.

No! You are not dead. You may have been dormant for a season. The devil tried to convince you that your spirit would never be resurrected and come back to life. *But the same spirit that raised Christ from the dead dwells inside you!*

Satan should have taken you completely out when he did his work on you, but he couldn't. Just like a boxer who gets up even after he has fallen on the canvas with the wind completely knocked out of him, you have refused to stay down. You got your wind back. If not, I pray this book puts a wind in you!

The past season of canceled church gatherings is over. We meet now with a comeback of God's people who have gotten their second wind. The reason the gathering was attacked in 2020 was because the enemy knows what is released when God's people gather! *The* ruach *of God is going to flood every faithful church.* The gifted and fancy will not replace the good and faithful. The remnant of God is much bolder now. We have had our senses exercised and our swords sharpened. It's a new day, and we are fighting differently. We will not bow to the attempts to silence us, shutter us, manipulate us, discourage us, or depress us. We will swing fists in the Spirit.

Satan needs to know something about this emerging Church that is gathering on the heels of this attack. We're not sitting around, soaking in tears of the past. We're planning our revenge! All the trouble he put us through only made us stronger. I want to *publicly* thank the enemy for making the Church sit down and take a look at our inventory. Now that we have emerged, we may be a lean bird in the wilderness—but this is better than being a fat bird in a cage!

This last season did not make sense to us, but this new season will not make sense to our enemy. Why? Because you shouldn't be blessed, but you're going to be blessed. You shouldn't be healed, but you're going to be healed. You shouldn't be free, but you're free. You shouldn't be alive, but you're alive; you should have no peace, but you will know peace. The offense couldn't stop you, the breaking couldn't block you, and the hurt couldn't hinder you! You are back up, with a firm grip, ready to readjust your focus and take a swing at this giant. You got your wind back! Heaven is backing you up and cheering you on as you make it back up on your feet in the ring of life.

Church, we are not on the ropes, and we are not down on the canvas. We have our second wind, and we are ready to eradicate our enemies.

Don't Stop at Structure, Prophesy to the Wind

God lifted up Ezekiel in the Spirit, that watchman who carried the trumpet of God in his mouth. He set him in a valley full of bones and told him to walk around them, taking inventory. While this specifically symbolizes the house of Israel, there is prophetic insight concerning the times in which we live as well.

Somewhere, something happened to that dead army! They stopped in a valley. David tells us in Psalm 23 that when we find ourselves in the valley of the shadow of death, we need to make sure we continue to walk through it. The important word is to "walk." God never called you to stay in a temporary season.

Secondly, God told Ezekiel to walk around the bones and assess them. They were dry, disconnected, fragmented, and lifeless. Then God asked him, "Can these bones live?"

While Ezekiel's answer was, "Only You know," God showed him how those bones would come forth: "Prophesy! Raise your voice, Ezekiel!"

And that's what He's telling us today. He calls for us to raise our voices in the midst of dead and dry bones. It's one thing to speak life when you're surrounded by life, but can you speak life when death surrounds you? *The key to being a voice for God is speaking into the future while looking at the present.* We certainly cannot speak to the future while focused on the past.

So Ezekiel prophesied! The first thing he saw was structure, then flesh. Do you know you can have an incredible system, structure, and even *strength*, but you still can't move without spirit? That sounds like a lot of churches in today's culture. They shut out the moving of the Spirit. God wants a second wind delivered by the prophetic among us. He is asking His voices to do that at this very moment in time! Speak again. This time, don't speak to the bones, speak to the wind!

If we want to see this powerful movement of God, the prophetic voice must shift from speaking to people to speaking to the *ruach* of God. Prophesy again—this time not to man, but to the wind.

After he prophesied the *second wind*—the *ruach* of God—upon the bones, Ezekiel saw an army. Not just any army, but "an exceedingly great" army. Only when the spirit came did the bones and flesh in the valley become an army.

Ezekiel prophesied to the four winds. This is what the Church is about to experience through this prophetic release. Your voice is going to release something when you prophesy like Ezekiel to the north, east, west, and south winds.

- The north wind drives storms away and reveals what is hidden and reserved (Job 37:9, 21–22).
- The east wind wipes out your enemy (Exodus 10:13; Psalm 48:7; Jeremiah 18:17).
- The west wind cleans the house (Exodus 10:19).
- The south wind speaks of provision, power, and fire (Numbers 11:31; Psalm 78:26; Acts 28:13; Luke 12:55).

My pastor, Joseph Morgan, once preached a powerful message about the doldrums—an atmospherical condition in which ocean-going ships are becalmed because there is no wind and no waves. When stuck in the doldrums, captains and sailors would utilize the time to repair and maintain the ship. *That is exactly what happened in 2020. The wind was stopped for a season and for a reason.* The ship of Zion had to be cleaned up. Many people jumped ship out of fear or inconvenience, but God was using voices to fire warning shots across the bow of the ship of Zion. "Get this place cleaned up, because the wind is about to blow."

The north, south, east, and west winds are called trade winds because they direct storm and ocean currents, and the captains of ships loaded with merchandise for trade would use them to get to their destinations faster. The trade winds are reliable winds even though they may be connected to storms.

There is a prevailing wind coming upon the Body of Christ through the prophetic unction and activation of a generation like Ezekiel's. The Church is loaded with precious cargo, and we plan to deliver it! We have navigated our way through ruthless pirates, shady smugglers, and enemy navies that still plan to take us out, but we are more prepared than ever before. The ship is clean, lean, and ready to sail. The ropes are secure, and the decks have been swabbed. The rudder (tongue) has been tuned to steer!

The second wind utilizes the power of the storm to move! It reveals what is hidden, wipes out enemies, cleans the house, and provides power and fire. This prophetic word causes the ship of Zion to become unstuck! Open your mouth and prophesy. Raise your voice to the winds. Pray in the Spirit and release the trade winds of faith. Here come the Voices of Revival. Set your sails back up!

Revival comes from repentance, not the other way around! The word "refreshing" means "revival"—a catching back of your breath. A wind! A *second wind*, to be exact, a "re"-freshing (Acts 3:19).

When the Holy Spirit came upon Jesus after His baptism, it came in the form of a dove. When the Holy Spirit came upon the Church, it came in the form of fire and the sound of a mighty wind. That famous day of Pentecost in Acts 2—the birth of the Church—is where we need to return. We need our wind, we need our fire, and we need to make a sound! The Church must not shut out the wind of God blowing in our lives and through our churches.

The Wind Represents Cleansing

In the sermon I mentioned earlier, Joseph Morgan also said, "When the wind stops blowing, things stop separating."

Wind is a powerful tool. In both the Old and New Testaments, it was used to separate the kernels from the chaff when grain was harvested. The second wind upon the Body of Christ will do the same. God has sent another wind of the Holy Spirit for those who will reach out and grab hold of it. This will require a separation.

The wind also reveals. We find this in Jesus's parable about the wheat and the tares. The text doesn't literally say this, but the meaning is there.

> The kingdom of heaven is like a man who sowed good seed in his field; but while men slept, his enemy came and sowed tares among the wheat and went his way. But when the grain had sprouted and produced a crop, then the tares also appeared. So the servants of the owner came and said to him, "Sir, did you not sow good seed in your field? How then does it have tares?" He said to them, "An enemy has done this." The servants said to him, "Do you want us then to go and gather them up?" But he said, "No, lest while you gather up the tares you also uproot the wheat with them. Let both grow together until the harvest, and at the time of harvest I will say to the reapers, 'First gather together the tares and bind them in bundles to burn them, but gather the wheat into my barn.'" (Matthew 13:24–30)

Isn't it interesting that the enemy comes when we sleep? When we are inactive, idle, and not watching for the enemy's attempt to find a foothold in our lives, he shows up—sowing seed in the fields of our families, lives, and society. But his day of reckoning is coming.

Jesus said not to take the tares out early for the sake of not hurting the wheat. To understand this parable, you have to understand wheat and tares. *They look identical* until harvest time. The difference is the wheat grows a stout head of fruit. Even though the tare looks like wheat, it doesn't produce fruit, but you can only see this when the wind begins to blow. As the wind blows, the ones with the fruit bow, but the ones without fruit will stand erect, rebelling against the wind.

Here is the prophetic insight about why the second wind is blowing. My wife, who pastors alongside me, prophetically spoke over the Body of Christ that we are in a "revealing and releasing" of good and evil. That means the wind is blowing and the harvest is here to reveal what is and what is not of God.

The second wind is blowing upon those who want the movement of the Spirit to meld with the power of His Word. And if it is harvest time, we need to understand what this means. I believe it is the eleventh hour. The clock is counting down every day, and God is looking for people to go out into His field, ready to reap the harvest.

CHAPTER 15

THE CALL FOR A VOICE

God Is Calling You!

Now the boy Samuel ministered to the LORD before Eli. And the word of the LORD was rare in those days; there was no widespread revelation. And it came to pass at that time, while Eli was lying down in his place, and when his eyes had begun to grow so dim that he could not see, and before the lamp of God went out in the tabernacle of the LORD where the ark of God was, and while Samuel was lying down, that the LORD called Samuel. And he answered, "Here I am!" So he ran to Eli and said, "Here I am, for you called me."

And he said, "I did not call; lie down again." And he went and lay down.

Then the LORD called yet again, "Samuel!"

So Samuel arose and went to Eli, and said, "Here I am, for you called me." He answered, "I did not call, my son; lie down again." (Now Samuel did not yet know the LORD, nor was the word of the LORD yet revealed to him.)

And the LORD called Samuel again the third time. So he arose and went to Eli, and said, "Here I am, for you did call me."

Then Eli perceived that the LORD had called the boy. Therefore Eli said to Samuel, "Go, lie down; and it shall be, if He calls you, that you must say, 'Speak, LORD, for Your servant hears.'" So Samuel went and lay down in his place.

Now the LORD came and stood and called as at other times, "Samuel! Samuel!"

And Samuel answered, "Speak, for Your servant hears."

Then the LORD said to Samuel: "Behold, I will do something in Israel at which both ears of everyone who hears it will tingle. In that day I will perform against Eli all that I have spoken concerning his house, from beginning to end. For I have told him that I will judge his house forever for the iniquity which he knows, because his sons made themselves vile, and he did not restrain them. And therefore I have sworn to the house of Eli that the iniquity of Eli's house shall not be atoned for by sacrifice or offering forever."

So Samuel lay down until morning, and opened the doors of the house of the LORD. And Samuel was afraid to tell Eli the vision. Then Eli called Samuel and said, "Samuel, my son!"

He answered, "Here I am."

And he said, "What is the word that the LORD spoke to you? Please do not hide it from me. God do so to you, and more also, if you hide anything from me of all the things that He said to you." Then Samuel told him everything, and hid nothing from him. And he said, "It is the LORD. Let Him do what seems good to Him."

So Samuel grew, and the LORD was with him and let none of his words fall to the ground. (1 Samuel 3:1–19)

The Changing of the Guard

I once had the privilege of going to Virginia's Arlington National Cemetery during the changing of the guard at the Tomb of the Unknown Soldier. These guards have been employed from 1937 to today to stand watch over this tomb 24 hours a day, 7 days a week, 365 days a year. It is one of the most protected places in the nation. Guards are chosen through rigorous testing. Only 10 percent of those who apply make it. On average, 10 per year are chosen to be the elite, the best of the best out of thousands of applicants.

I watched the active guard march from left to right, right to left, twenty-one steps symbolizing the highest honor in the military, clicking his heels, facing the unknown soldier's tomb, and saluting him. The respect he's given shows his value. The guards do this over and over, with precision, weathering any elements.

Unmoved by the crowd, these elite soldiers march with no other care or concern than to bring honor to the unknown soldier and guard the tomb. There are YouTube videos showing that the guards have remained unmoved by hurricanes, blizzards, earthquakes, and lightning strikes—even the 9/11 attacks. If someone breaches the chain cordoning the tomb away from the public, the guard will break his repetitious rhythm to assume an attack position and give a strong verbal warning. The guards are not to be messed with.

During the changing of the guard, everyone watching is told to stand and be quiet. A high level of respect is demanded during this ceremony. The active guard continues to march as the head guard comes out to inspect the upcoming guard. He inspects his weapon with such detailed accuracy that even the slightest bit of dirt on any part of the gun means disqualification. He then looks the soldier over from top to bottom and left to right to make sure his uniform is free of any lint, dirt, or wrinkle before he allows him to move. He will then walk behind the soldier and inspect him from behind to make sure that everything has been cleaned, pressed, and is in place. Once that soldier is inspected, the head guard begins to walk with the upcoming guard in order to transfer the responsibilities to be the watchman for the next shift. It is a solemn and sacred ceremony and is to be treated as such.

We are in a season of the changing of the guard. Many out-pourings are happening to those who are calling out for more of God—the watchmen and -women who see the enemy coming and whose response is complete abandonment of unrighteousness and a hunger for God's presence. College campuses, churches, and cities are igniting with new voices that are emerging. Many previously great voices have faded away, but the anointing they carried is here for the next generation of watchmen on the walls. They are inspected by God Himself. They have had rigorous training in their private lives. They have been inspected to make sure the integrity of the Word of the Lord remains true and in effect in their ministries. They stand on guard as the commencement begins for them to take their rightful place as watchmen.

The difference is that we are not serving an unknown person, but the King of kings and the Lord of lords. These watchmen are the remnant of God. They are not moved by trends or tactics, storms or circumstances, praise or criticism. Their objective is to repeat righteousness until they are relieved by death. They are relentless and anointed to preserve the greatest book of all time, the Bible. The spiritual guards are moving into position to rebuff anyone who disrespects the authenticity or veracity of God's Word.

We are undaunted and remain unalarmed by the culture's demand for change. We stand and march with the highest honor given to our God. Our voice resonates with the same sentiments as that of the last guard because we are trained by the same head guard, Jesus Christ.

God did not call you out of the world. He called you out of the *systems* of the world. Your voice is here to govern and maintain a standard—a call to guard what has been given to you, holding fast to sound words. Jesus even prayed that His disciples wouldn't be taken out of the world but would be protected while they were here representing the Kingdom of God.

Samuel was dedicated as a child to serve God. His mother gave him to the high priest, Eli, when he was a boy to serve by performing menial tasks in the Temple. As time passed and Samuel grew, the Bible says the lamps in the Temple were not being kept lit under Eli's compromised leadership. The scripture makes two very strong statements right before the changing of the guard from

Eli to Samuel: "The Word of the Lord was rare," and "there was no revelation." Eli was undoubtedly a good man who served the Lord, but he would not deal with his two sons, who continued to provoke God with their sinful ways. He had failed to take his position seriously enough to fulfill the duties of being the watchman of his generation.

This was the scene right before the changing of the regimes. The fire was going out. People were beginning to do what was right in their own eyes without any constraint or holy direction.

The lamp of God in our day is sputtering out as well. Without the lamp, the work of God cannot continue. The lamp is fed by oil, which represents the Holy Spirit.

Listen! What's coming up in this world must be met by people who are called to carry the fire of God. Chaos is created when leaders lose their fire to lead. God's people becoming unaccountable is unacceptable to Him. Just like Eli's sons, they will refuse correction and turn away from conviction. When this happens, the lights will dim and the voice of God will provide no widespread revelation. Darkness will take over.

The last twenty years have been filled with communicators, motivational speakers, and inspirational coaches who have not spoken the heart of God, but rather tickled the ears of men. It has left people confused about what God's Word says. Now there's a revolution, a changing of the guard that's unfolding, and people need a voice that speaks on God's behalf—not just in the pulpit, but also in their homes and in the streets, schools, and government. The Asbury Revival, as well as other outpourings, have spawned a great hunger in the remnant to boldly go forth in a new season. Another regime is emerging. God's remnant in this world is now relighting the flames of revival, burning the lights brightly concerning God's Word and righteous living.

Samuel heard God calling him, but he was confused. He thought Eli was calling. Eli's call represents the voice of a closing season of bad decisions. When God raises us up to be the voices of a next generation, we must be careful that we don't assume the characteristics of a previous generation that spoke with compromise. Not everybody from the previous generation has spoken with compromise, but we have a natural tendency to go back to the way things have always been, even when God is asking for something new. Every person has a tendency to hit the reset button when challenges beset him or transition is underway. Samuel was trained to work in the ministry but not to hear the voice of the Lord. And he was definitely not trained to speak. That was Eli's role.

But God was done speaking through Eli, whose stubbornness and refusal to confront the evils of his day caused his ministry to tolerate evil. So God called Samuel.

Samuel went to Eli and said, "Here I am."

Eli said, "I didn't call you."

How prophetic those words were. *God* was calling Samuel, and He didn't even bother to speak to Eli about it. Finally, Samuel understood that God was calling him to the forefront. He was about to anoint him as a prophet and use his voice. Samuel delivered that message to Eli, and from that moment on, as the Bible specifically says, none of his words fell to the ground!

It's one thing for you to trust God; it's another thing for God to trust you. When He does, He will not allow your words to fall to the ground. He backs up those who choose to follow His call on their lives. What a place to be—the place where God knows you will speak for Him. It's not an easy place, but it is so rewarding to know God backs up your words because He has called you to be a resonant voice for Him in this generation.

Read on. You're not just reading information, you're reading *impartation!*

God is calling your voice to the forefront. Just as Samuel received a call to confront those who were comfortable in their sin, so will the remnant of God who raise their voice in the generation ahead. Raise your voice! He's calling you! Go after God in this season of opportunity He is giving us. The winds of revival and outpouring are on us. Take hold of it and claim it for yourself, your family, your city, and your nation!

CHAPTER 16

IT'S ABOUT TIME

Hell's Outrage Will Be Met with Heaven's Outpouring

I t's about time!

I love what Pastor Samuel Rodriguez has been saying: "THE TIME HAS COME!" God has an appointed time! This is what the Old Testament prophet Joel spoke about.

The Asbury Revival could not have come at a better time. It broke out spontaneously on February 8, 2023, when about two dozen college students in Kentucky gathered after a typical (some would say not very inspiring) chapel service and began to call upon the name of the Lord. Over the next two weeks, some fifty thousand Christian worshipers, celebrity pastors, and onlookers flocked to the university chapel to experience God moving firsthand. A livestream of the services garnered more than fifty-five million views, and social media users around the world shared videos that have spawned a spiritual awakening that continues to gain steam. There was no denying that God was in this!

It's worth noting that the revival broke out just three days after an unholy performance of satanic worship was broadcast nationwide on the annual Grammy Awards telecast. It was almost as if God was letting the world know that the answer to such wickedness and open devil worship (which was seen by 12.4 million Americans) was a small remnant calling out, that then turned into tens of millions watching—and sparked hotspots of revival on other college campuses across the nation and around the world.

An epic showdown is taking place right before our eyes. While this is the first of many showdowns to come, this one is about God releasing a fresh wind of revival through the remnant of believers. Isaiah 60:1–2 says that when darkness comes, so does glory. When we get up, God shows up!

> Arise, shine;
> For your light has come!
> And the glory of the LORD is risen upon you.
> For behold, the darkness shall cover the earth,
> And deep darkness the people;
> But the LORD will arise over you,
> And His glory will be seen upon you.

When we arise, God arises over us. This epic showdown that we are seeing is a battle of good and evil. God is pouring out His presence and power on those arising!

Did you notice who God used to start the revival? A handful of college students, still being educated, who aren't celebrities with huge followings on their social media pages. What caused such an epic move of the Holy Spirit? Hunger and repentance!

Revival does not have a recipe. If it did, then we would know exactly how to have revival every time we want one. However, revival does have a catalyst—something that propels a thing to begin! A catalyst is an agent that provokes significant change. Repentance and hunger are the catalysts for revival.

Revival is not a string of services or a special event we plan. It often does not fit in our schedules, and it has a way of challenging our religious routines. But that's what a remnant does: We step outside the routine and chase after God in a time when He can be found.

Isaiah 55:6 says to "seek the LORD while he may be found, call upon him while he is near." Acts 3:19 says to "Repent therefore and be converted, that your sins may be blotted out, so that times of refreshing may come from the presence of the Lord."

We are in a time right now when God is near. I believe the outpouring of God is now upon the earth. Why? Because darkness also is upon the earth, and Isaiah 60 speaks of "a deep darkness" that descends upon the people. It's actually the darkness that reveals to us how badly God is needed in our nations.

The Greek language has two words for "time": *chronos* and *kairos*. *Chronos* is the sequential ticking of time, its chronological measurement. *Kairos*, however, speaks of a season or opportunity. Simply put, *chronos* is the measuring of time, whereas *kiaros* is a measure of God in a space of time. We are in the time when the Lord desires to visit His people!

It Will Happen at the Same Time

Matthew 24 will be met with Joel 2 in the Last Days. Matthew 24 is where Jesus's desciples ask, "What will be the sign of Your coming and of the end of the age?" He gives them multiple markers that will help them know when the end of the age is coming. He says things like "Many will come in My name, but they are not Me. You will hear of wars and rumors of wars, nations will rise against nations, races and kingdoms will be at odds, there will be famine, pestilence, earthquakes in various places, and these will all be the signs of the beginning of sorrow. Lawlessness will abound and the love of many will grow cold. The Gospel of the Kingdom will be preached, and then the end will come."

It's almost scary when you read it! All of these things happening at once. I do believe we are living in the last seconds of the last days. However, there is another passage of Scripture that says something amazing will happen simultaneously.

Joel 2 tells us God will pour out His spirit "on all flesh." Peter referenced that verse in Acts 2:17–21 when he said:

> And it shall come to pass in the last days, says God,
> That I will pour out of My Spirit on all flesh;
> Your sons and your daughters shall prophesy,
> Your young men shall see visions,
> Your old men shall dream dreams.
> And on My menservants and on My maidservants
> I will pour out My Spirit in those days;
> And they shall prophesy.
> I will show wonders in heaven above

And signs in the earth beneath:
Blood and fire and vapor of smoke.
The sun shall be turned into darkness,
And the moon into blood,
Before the coming of the great and awesome day of the
LORD.
And it shall come to pass
That whoever calls on the name of the LORD
Shall be saved.

The verbiage that Jesus used in speaking of "the last days" is the same verbiage Peter uses. Jesus speaks of all of the markers in the world concerning that time, and Peter speaks of all the markers in the Church. While the world is reeling with lawlessness, cold hearts, wars, and deception, the Church will go into a season of revival, the Spirit pouring out, daughters and sons prophesying, young men seeing visions, and old men dreaming dreams. There will be a huge deluge of the power of the Holy Spirit upon God's people.

These are not sequential events. They will happen simultaneously. The world will be on fire one way, and the Church will be on fire in another. Darkness will be on the earth, but so will God's glory! That means there will be a definitive line drawn, and you must choose which side you want to be on and where you want to go.

I believe Joel 2 is God's manifesto! This may sound crazy to you, but prophetic things often sound that way. I sought the Lord on this. He led me to Joel 2 and said, "Look at the verses, and align them with the years." For instance, Joel 2:20 would represent 2020, and so on. Here is what I saw in the Spirit:

- 2:20: the plague of a northern army
- 2:21: "fear not"
- 2:22: open pastures are springing up, trees are bearing fruit, the fig and vine yield strength
- 2:23: outpouring
- 2:24: overflow
- 2:25: restoration
- 2:26: having plenty and being satisfied
- 2:27: "You will know that I am God"
- 2:28–29: "I will pour out"
- 2:30: signs and wonders
- 2:31: He's coming
- 2:32: The remnant is marked

Many believe the "northern army," which Joel mentions several times, was a great plague that came from locusts. The first nine verses discuss this army. Then Joel 2:25 says, "I will restore to you the years that the swarming locust has eaten . . . my great army that I sent against you." There was a great plague referenced in Joel 2:20; this is exactly what happened to us in 2020 all over the nations. A plague—a pandemic.

Verse 21 says that the people should not fear. That's exactly what we experienced in 2021: fear gripped our hearts because of the pandemic. In verse 22, again God says, "Do not be afraid," but with this declaration, He says things will begin to open back up. That's exactly what happened in 2022; people were still gripped by fear, but at the same time, businesses and churches begin to open back up. It also happened to be the last year of a seven-year cycle in the Hebrew calendar, which is called a *shmita*. That means a new seven-year cycle arrived in 2023—and notice how the narrative changes in Joel 2:23! *The next seven years will bring great harvest and blessings!*

I truly believe over the next seven years, the Body of Christ will see outpouring, overflowing, restoration, satisfaction, and God being made known to *all*. It's TIME! It's time to turn our fear into great faith.

The culmination of Matthew 24 and Joel 2 is found in Isaiah 60: Darkness is on the face of the earth, but the glory of God will always be stronger than any evil being exalted!

What Now?

What is our response to these two passages? How do we raise our voice in such calamitous times? We must first repent, as Acts 3 says, which means to simply change our minds to line up with God's—examine ourselves and change the way we think and the way we walk. Go after God, and allow His times of refreshing to so overtake us so that evil does not shake us and we may be firmly fixed in Jesus Christ.

I believe the outpouring of the Holy Spirit is upon us! In the last days, the Bible tells us Satan will spend seven years deceiving the nations. Don't think for a second that Satan is going to get his seven years in before the Church gets theirs! I truly believe starting in 2023, we'll experience the greatest seven years of outpouring that the nations have ever seen.

While the Euphrates River is drying up as we speak—Revelation 16:12 says it will be completely dry before the Battle of Armageddon takes place—and the world is being shaken by pandemics, diseases, disasters, and earthquakes, we are poised for the End Time Revival. We are not in the Tribulation; we are at "the beginning of sorrows" (Matthew 24:8).

Look up, look up! The way Jesus left is the same way He's coming back! This is the season when we thrust the sickle into the harvest and go after the greatest outpouring the world has ever seen. It's our time of refreshing!

Win the lost at any cost—on street corners, in chapels, on the rooftops! Shout out the name of Jesus! His name is greater than any other name! There is a heavy rain of God's presence pouring out! It is happening, and this is an exciting time to be alive! So raise your voice. Be *fully convinced* that God has you on this earth at this time for a purpose! Rally with the remnant, become loud in the eleventh hour, cry out, ask God for a second wind, become the emergent divergent, and let's watch God move on our behalf! This is the time! It's the moment you were created for!

Acknowledgments

First and foremost, to my God! He has been faithful to me in ways I cannot even begin to explain.

I want to thank the people of Worship With Wonders Church for hearing my voice every week as I searched out the heart of God from this burden I received over these last few years. Your continued support for DeLana and me, as your pastors, has meant the world to us.

To our children, Brooklyn, Lyncoln, Kendall, and Jocelyn. To have all four of you working in full-time ministry alongside Mom and me has thrilled us more than you know. You are a great inspiration to us as we raise our voices daily. Your generation is worth the investments made! I love and appreciate all of you and the strong ways your voices are developing for God. Much of the joy I have comes from seeing all of you walking in the destinies God has for you. You make the father in me proud. I love all of you!

My mother, Sue Rutherford. You pray, encourage, speak into my life, and love me as well as all my family. I love and honor you. You are the epitome of what it means to be a mom, and I love you dearly for that. Thank you for all the years you have celebrated the voice God has given me. To my dad, who has gone on to be with Jesus, I have this voice because of you. Dad, you were such a rock. I miss you daily. I am grateful you have helped steer my life. Your words still echo in me when I speak. I pray this book honors the legacy you gave to us. Until we meet again.

Notes

Chapter 2: Cry Out

1. William Booth Quotations, Christianity 201, May 21, 2012, https://christianity 201.wordpress.com/2012/05/21/william-booth-quotations.

Chapter 3: The Church Is in Trouble

1. "How Long Should Church Services and Sermons Be?," National Association of Evangelicals, July 5, 2017, https://www.nae.org/long-church-services-sermons.
2. See Jacque St. Jude Johnson Sr., "Dr. Myles Monroe—The Kingdom of Ignorance (Darkness)," YouTube, August 28, 2022, https://youtu.be/eU3QFSySsWk.
3. Mark Munter, "Soldiers (Original 1982) B. H. Clendennen," YouTube, April 17, 2018, https://youtu.be/tUFZC3QDiWI.
4. "William Booth Quotes," Goodreads, https://www.goodreads.com/author/quotes/21870904.William_Booth.

Chapter 5: Clean the House

1. Clifford Denton, "Testing Prophecies Together: Smith Wigglesworth's 1947 Prophecy," Prophetic Insights, May 6, 2016, https://www.prophecytoday. uk/study/prophetic-insights/item/389-testing-prophecies-together-smith-wigglesworth-s-1947-prophecy.html.
2. "One in Three Practicing Christians Has Stopped Attending Church during COVID-19," Barna, July 8, 2020, https://www.barna.com/research/new-sunday-morning-part-2/.
3. Jeffrey M. Jones, "U.S. Church Membership Falls Below Majority for First Time," Gallup, March 29, 2021, https://news.gallup.com/poll/341963/church-membership-falls-below-majority-first-time.aspx.
4. Bridget Sharkey, "Poll Suggests 76% of Americans across Most Religions Support LGBTQ Equality," Simplemost, April 19, 2021, https://www.10news. com/poll-76-religious-americans-support-lgbtq-rights.

Chapter 8: Rally the Remnant

1. Taylor Swift, "You Need to Calm Down," YouTube, June 17, 2019, https://youtu. be/Dkk9gvTmCXY.
2. See Israel A. Perez, "Music Video Breakdown: 'Montero (Call Me By Your Name)'," *The Harvard Crimson*, April 13, 2021, https://www.thecrimson.com/

article/2021/4/13/lil-nas-x-montero-mvb/; See also Oscar Holland and Jacqui Palumbo, "Lil Nas X's Unofficial 'Satan' Nikes Containing Human Blood Sell Out in under a Minute," CNN, March 29, 2021, https://www.cnn.com/style/article/lil-nas-x-mschf-satan-nike-shoes/index.html.

3. Nika Shakhnazarova, "Sam Smith, Kim Petras 'Unholy' Grammy Performance Sparks FCC Complaints," New York Post, February 11, 2023, https://nypost.com/2023/02/11/sam-smith-kim-petras-unholy-grammy-performance-sparks-fcc-complaints/.

4. Beyoncé, "Denial (Lemonade Poem, Part 2) Lyrics," Genius, 2016, https://genius.com/Beyonce-denial-lemonade-poem-part-2-lyrics.

5. Blue's Clues & You!, "The Blue's Clues Pride Parade Sing-Along Ft. Nina West!," YouTube, May 28, 2021, https://youtu.be/d4vHegf3WPU.

6. Jesse T. Jackson, "Ouija Board for Christians? 'The Holy Spirit Board' Sold on Amazon Advertises as 'Christian Religious Talking Board'," ChurchLeaders, November 11, 2022, https://churchleaders.com/news/438454-ouija-board-for-christians-the-holy-spirit-board-sold-on-amazon-advertises-as-christian-religious-talking-board.html.

7. A. W. Tozer, *The Tozer Pulpit: Selections from His Pulpit Ministry, Book 6* (Effingham, Illinois: Wingspread Publishers, 1994), 32.

Chapter 10: When Voices Go Missing

1. "Ezekiel 13:1–9," Matthew Henry's Concise Commentary, Biblehub.com, https://biblehub.com/commentaries/ezekiel/13-9.htm.

Chapter 11: And Men Loved the Darkness

1. Mister Retrops, "Spain Decriminalizes Sexual Relations with Animals as Long as There Is No Physical Injury That Requires a Veterinary Visit," Not the Bee, February 19, 2023, https://notthebee.com/article/spain-decriminalizes-sexual-relations-with-animals-as-long-as-there-is-no-physical-injury-that-requires-a-veterinary-visit.

Chapter 12: They/Them

1. Lindsey Dawson, Jennifer Kates, and MaryBeth Musumeci, "Youth Access to Gender Affirming Care: The Federal and State Policy Landscape," Kaiser Family Foundation, June 1, 2022, https://www.kff.org/other/issue-brief/youth-access-to-gender-affirming-care-the-federal-and-state-policy-landscape/.

2. Linda Poon, "'Ze' or 'They'? A Guide to Using Gender-Neutral Pronouns," Bloomberg News, September 28, 2015, https://www.bloomberg.com/news/articles/2015-09-28/-ze-or-they-a-guide-to-using-nonbinary-gender-neutral-pronouns; See also Toni Airaksinen, "College Lists 'ne,' 've,' 'ey' as Gender Neutral Pronouns," Campus Reform, March 1, 2018, https://www.campusreform.org/article?id=10583.